William Morris

Story Memory Myth

Published to accompany the exhibition at
Two Temple Place, London
28th October 2011 – 29th January 2012

Published in 2011 by Two Temple Place.
2 Temple Place,
London, WC2R 3BD

'Reading the Walls:
William Morris and the Art of Storytelling'

Story summaries by Madeleine Reid

A catalogue record for this publication
is available from the British Library

ISBN 978 0 9570628 0 1

Designed and produced by N/A.

Cover image:
'Love Leading the Pilgrim Through the Briars' from
The Romance of the Rose embroidered frieze.
Edward Burne-Jones and William Morris, 1874 - 82.
William Morris Gallery, London.

Foreword

William Morris: *Story, Memory, Myth*

The Bulldog Trust is immensely proud to launch, with this exhibition at Two Temple Place, a programme to provide the first exhibition space in London specifically to showcase works from museums and collections outside central London and across the country. We believe that support for these museums and galleries, through annual exhibitions and related events, is timely, worthwhile and thoroughly in keeping with the Trust's wider charitable purposes.

We hope that this programme will, over time, enable a wide range of museums and galleries outside London to extend their public profile and attract wider support. While many exhibitions originating in the major national institutions of London tour widely throughout the country, there is surprisingly little reciprocal flow. We are hoping to change that, to afford audiences here a view of the richness of these collections, to increase awareness of their holdings and to encourage visits. With the current reductions in government arts funding affecting organisations across the country, there could be no better time.

Two Temple Place is wholly owned by the Bulldog Trust. The Bulldog Trust is a grant-making charity which sponsors both new artistic initiatives, and young charities working in the social field which need a 'venture capital' approach to assist them in their formative years. The trustees of the Trust have been exploring how we could give this magnificent building the mission it deserves, ever since Two Temple Place was purchased for the Bulldog Trust in 1999.

Our customary approach, as a charity, is to ensure that everything we do adds value. Our aims in this project, consequently, are threefold: to mount important exhibitions that celebrate and raise awareness of the country's rich public treasures; to highlight the extraordinary environment of Two Temple Place as a space for display and to allow the public to feast their eyes on what Sir John Betjeman called 'one of the most attractive late-Victorian private houses in London'; and, finally, to encourage and provide opportunities for up-and-coming curatorial talent.

One important feature of the exhibition programme here is that there will be no charge for admission. We believe that if objects can be seen for free in their regional homes, no barriers should be placed in the path of those wishing to view them at Two Temple Place.

We are proud to collaborate with our first partner in this venture, the William Morris Gallery in Walthamstow, who have welcomed our approach and collaborated in this venture with great enthusiasm. We are extremely grateful to be working with them and to be able to show their remarkable but still too little-known collection at Two Temple Place. This first exhibition will, we believe, inspire more Londoners to make the short trip to Walthamstow to see the Morris Collection in its true home when the William Morris Gallery re-opens, following major refurbishment, in July 2012.

We are pleased to afford the curator, Dr Esmé Whittaker, the opportunity to research and select her first exhibition; we are well aware of the challenge of working within the splendid, ornate interiors of this building, and are impressed with the sensitivity with which she has brought together the exhibition and its particular space. Dr Whittaker was introduced to us by Martin Caiger-Smith, the Curatorial Adviser and her mentor on this project, who heads the Curating MA at The Courtauld Institute. We hope to maintain and build on this relationship with our neighbouring institution and to continue to provide much-needed opportunities for gifted young curators in all fields.

The magnificent Two Temple Place was built for the first Viscount Astor, William Waldorf, in the 1890s as his estate office and family pied à terre in London. The building was designed by the celebrated 19th-century architect John Loughborough Pearson, and was heavily influenced by Astor's love of literary and mythological characters and stories. This first such exhibition, *William Morris: Story, Memory, Myth*, is the perfect foil to the building. Exploring Morris's work through looking at the influence of literature and legend, it provides an intriguing new context in which to view his varied output. The contrast in style between the near-contemporary works of Morris and Pearson, and perhaps, in politics between Morris and the Astors, adds spice to the exhibition.

We are heavily indebted to all who have been involved in the development of this project for their support and advice. Besides those already mentioned, we would, in particular, like to thank our adviser David Barrie, Lorna Lee, Director of the William Morris Gallery in Walthamstow, and my fellow trustee Kim Panter Hoare.

And of course, without Richard Q Hoare OBE, the founder and main benefactor of the Bulldog Trust, who was behind the original visionary purchase of Two Temple Place, none of this would have been possible.

We hope you enjoy the exhibition.

Patrick Burgess

Chairman,
The Bulldog Trust.
October 2011

Reading the Walls:
William Morris and the Art of Storytelling

'In the fine time of art what the designer thought of was always in some way to appeal to the imagination; in other words, to tell some story, however imperfectly'.[1]

In 1874 William Morris and his close friend the artist Edward Burne-Jones began designing an embroidered frieze which would decorate the upper walls of the dining room at Rounton Grange, Northallerton, Yorkshire, a house that had been recently built by the architect Philip Webb. The embroidery depicts *The Romance of the Rose*, the 13th-century French dream debate over love which was known to Morris and Burne-Jones through a translation attributed to Geoffrey Chaucer. Standing in the dining room at Rounton Grange, gazing at the long expanse of embroidery above the fireplace, the viewer would have seen another encounter between a figure and a decorated wall (Fig. 1). The first panel of the frieze depicts the moment when the narrator 'saw suddenly a garden, both wide and long, completely enclosed with a high wall with battlements, painted and carved with rich scenes'.[2] Both the author of *The Romance of the Rose* and William Morris recognised the potential of the decorated surface of a wall to tell a tale.

The wall surface, whether painted, hung with textiles or inset with stained glass, had the power to make storytelling a communal experience, an experience which was close to the oral tradition of exchanging tales. Morris longed for a noble and splendid building

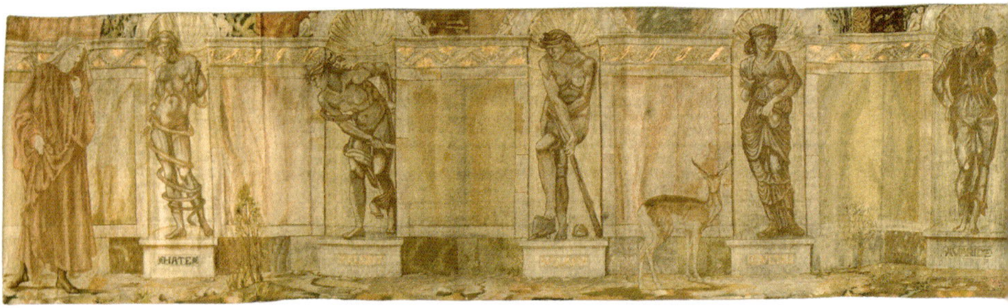

Fig.1. Edward Burne-Jones and William Morris, 'The Pilgrim Studying Images of the Vices on the exterior of the Garden of Idleness' from *The Romance of the Rose* embroidered frieze.

'duly ornamented so as to express the life and aspirations of the citizens…its mere decoration an epic wrought for the pleasure and education, not of the present generation only, but of many generations to come'.[3] This building would be created collaboratively. The stories told upon its walls would be shared by the whole community and, like a legend or folk tale, passed down through the generations. In his lectures, Morris reminds us that such a building once existed, that both the Greek temple and the Gothic church were not colourless and cold, but clad with 'a great epic, a story appealing to the hearts and minds of men'.[4] Through his designs for textiles, wallpapers, stained glass and ceramic tiles, Morris aimed to clad the walls with stories so that such a building could exist once again.

The Storyteller and The Craftsman

In his essay *The Storyteller* from 1936, the German philosopher and cutural critic Walter Benjamin explained the close relationship

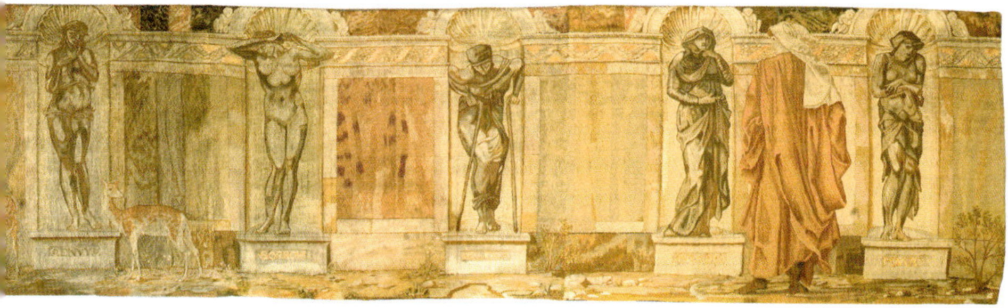

Linen embroidered with silks, wools and gold thread, 1874-82. Embroidered by Margaret Bell and her daughter Florence. William Morris Gallery, London.

between the craft and storytelling traditions.[5] He describes how the craftsman's workshop was the place where stories from the past and from faraway places were exchanged between the resident master craftsman and travelling journeymen. The stories were told as the craftsmen carried out their work, the rhythm of the words merging with the rhythm of their tools. Morris also believed that storytelling belonged within the craftsman's workshop. He often read aloud, in a rhythmic sing-song voice as Burne-Jones worked or uttered lines to himself under his breath while, with charcoal, brush or pencil, he composed a decorative design.

As both a poet and a decorative designer, Morris embodied the link between storytelling and craftsmanship. This dual role of poet and paper-maker or poet and printer caused confusion among the Victorian press. They wondered how Morris was capable of both and feared that his craft activities would distract him from his poetry. In 1893 a journalist from the *Daily Chronicle*, after a discussion about Morris's newly-founded private printing press, asked, 'Don't you think there is a danger of our losing a poet in the Kelmscott printer – that is, if he becomes too much a printer?' Morris's answer was simple: 'But if a man writes poetry it is a great advantage that he should do other work. His poetry will be better…'.[6] Morris did not see the writing of poetry as an isolated or sacrosanct activity but as one of many crafts. He famously proclaimed that, 'If a chap can't compose an epic poem while he's weaving tapestry…he had better shut up, he'll never do any good at all'.[7]

The Woodpecker tapestry (Fig.2), woven in 1885, is an example of Morris working simultaneously as a poet and a decorative designer. It is one of a series of tapestries for which Morris composed lines of verse, verses which in 1891 were published in his book *Poems by the Way*.[8] The tapestry depicts a tree, its trunk entwined with swirling acanthus leaves and its branches heavy with fruit. It could almost act as an illustration of Morris's statement about the potential of tapestry as a craft: 'You really may almost turn your wall into a rose-hedge or a deep forest, for its materials and general capabilities almost compel us to fashion plane above plane of rich, crisp, and varying foliage with bright blossoms, or strange birds showing through the intervals'.[9]

Two birds sit in the dense branches of the tree; one of them is a woodpecker. The significance of this bird is suggested by the inscription on the scrolls which form the top and bottom borders of the woven panel. The verse reads:

'I once a King and chief
Now am the tree-bark's thief,
Ever 'twixt trunk and leaf
Chasing the prey.'

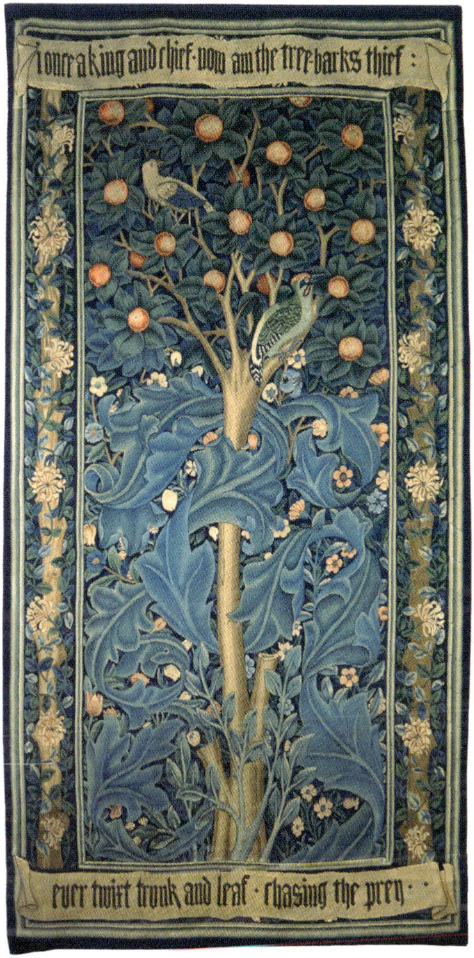

Fig.2. William Morris, *The Woodpecker* tapestry.
Woven wool and silk on a cotton warp, 1885. Morris & Co.
William Morris Gallery, London

It refers to the story of Picus, King of Ausonia, who according to Ovid's *Metamorphoses* was transformed into a woodpecker by the goddess Circe because he did not return her love. Picus, which is the Latin name for woodpecker, was destined to spend his days angrily pecking at the tree bark with his hard beak.[10] Morris depicts this narrative as a single decorative motif, the layer upon layer of foliage and blossoms evoking the woodland thicket where Picus becomes trapped. The verse, with its riddle-like form, adds another layer of decoration and mystery to the woven panel rather than literally explaining its subject.

Sharing Stories

Morris was nostalgic for an age when communities gathered together in order to share stories. He recreated this practice in his own life during his student years at Oxford when he and his friends would gather in their college rooms and read aloud from medieval chronicles and modern poetry. Throughout his life he would continue to read his own poetry out loud to his friends and family. It was this act of communal storytelling that provided the structure for his famous narrative poem *The Earthly Paradise*, in which a group of wanderers and their hosts meet twice a month to exchange medieval and classical tales.[11] This is the same exchange between travellers and natives which Benjamin describes – the interpenetration of 'the lore of faraway places, such as a much-travelled man brings home, with the lore of the past, as it best reveals itself to natives of a place'. [12]

Benjamin believed that the best written texts are those that differ least 'from the speech of the many nameless storytellers', and Morris was also drawn to texts that were close to their oral storytelling roots.[13] For example, Morris preferred the versions of the Arthurian legends in Thomas Malory's late 15th-century text, *Le Morte Darthur*, rather than Alfred Tennyson's popular Victorian version, *Idylls of the King* (1859-85). As Christine Poulson has explained, the directness and sparseness of Malory's prose style appealed to Morris and was itself 'a legacy of the oral tradition in which *Le Morte Darthur* is strongly rooted...

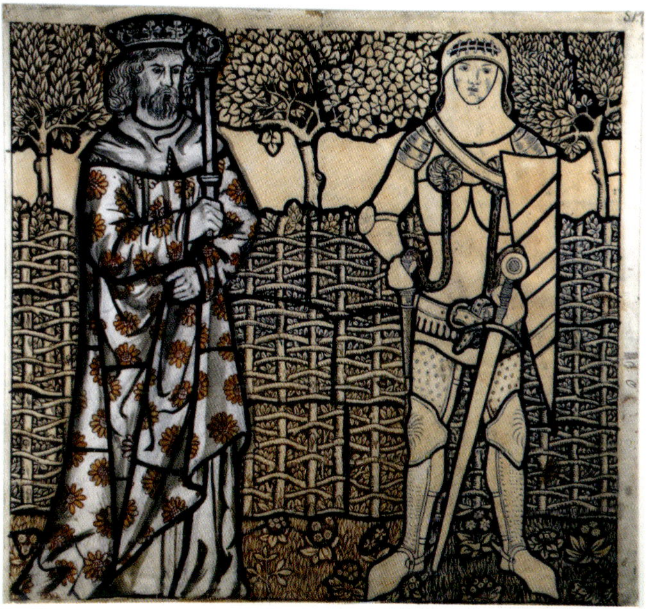

Fig.3. William Morris, design for *King Arthur and Sir Launcelot* stained-glass panel from *The Story of Tristram and Isoude* series. Black and sepia washes and pencil on paper, 1862. William Morris Gallery, London

The culture within which Malory was writing was still one in which people were much more accustomed to listening to stories than to reading them'.[14] This same directness is evident in the series of thirteen stained glass panels depicting the Arthurian story of Tristram and Isoude which were created collaboratively for the Yorkshire home of the merchant Walter Dunlop (Fig.3).

The designers included Burne-Jones and Dante Gabriel Rossetti, but it was Morris who decided upon the placement of the lead lines, providing a clear outline for the figures and their simple gestures. It was also Morris who selected which episodes would be depicted in the stained glass panels in order to convey the essence of the story. He did this by writing a short text in which he 'sorts out the tangled strands of Malory's story, and weaves it into an intelligible whole, annotating the margin with brief suggestions of pictorial possibilities'.[15] Each panel has a border of text beneath it, a summary of the action similar to that used in Malory's chapter headings. But the panels are as much a piece of decoration as a depiction of a narrative episode. This is exemplified by Morris's portrayal of King Arthur with his flower-patterned costume and Sir Launcelot with his embellished armour standing against the background of a tightly woven wattle fence. They demonstrate Morris's aim to make stained glass, not a series of pictures 'but rather pieces of ornamental glazing which, while decorating the buildings of which they formed a part, should also tell stories in a simple straightforward manner'.[16]

The story of Tristram and Isoude was Morris's favourite part of the Arthurian legends. He saw the saga, which is mentioned in Welsh folklore, as being part of his inheritance, writing 'all my literary life

I have been deeply moved by that Cycle of Romance, as indeed I ought to be, being myself Welsh of kin'.[17] He appreciated stories that were part of a shared folk heritage. For example, the Afro-American folktales about Brer Rabbit had a particular relevance to Morris in the early 1880s as he began to align himself with the Socialist cause. They are stories about a trickster, a common character in folklore who was able through his quick wits to get himself out of difficult situations. As Robert Hemenway explains, 'He embodies a revolutionary consciousness which says that one need not accept the world as it is, that any individual, working with the mother wit at hand, can change things'.[18] With this revolutionary nature it is little wonder that Morris, before reading his Socialist polemic *A Dream of John Ball* out loud to his family, gave a reading of *Brer Rabbit*.[19]

Morris encountered the Brer Rabbit folktales through J. C. Harris's collection of stories *Uncle Remus His Songs and His Sayings* which was published in 1881. According to Morris's daughter, May, this book and the textile design it inspired (Fig.4) was 'much loved in the family'.[20] The multiplied image of the rabbit that forms the textile design gives a sense not only of the abundance of Brer Rabbit tales but also the trickery of this cunning creature. It was the rabbit's knowledge of his own environment that allowed him to outwit his foes and in Morris's textile he is shown as being completely at home in his woodland setting encircled by scrolling leaves. There is an equality between the rabbits, birds, flowers, leaves and oak trees; they are all part of the same pattern which was block-printed using a bleaching agent on indigo dyed cloth. Morris and his family were pleased with the result. They 'considered that Brer Rab was duly honoured by this representation'.[21]

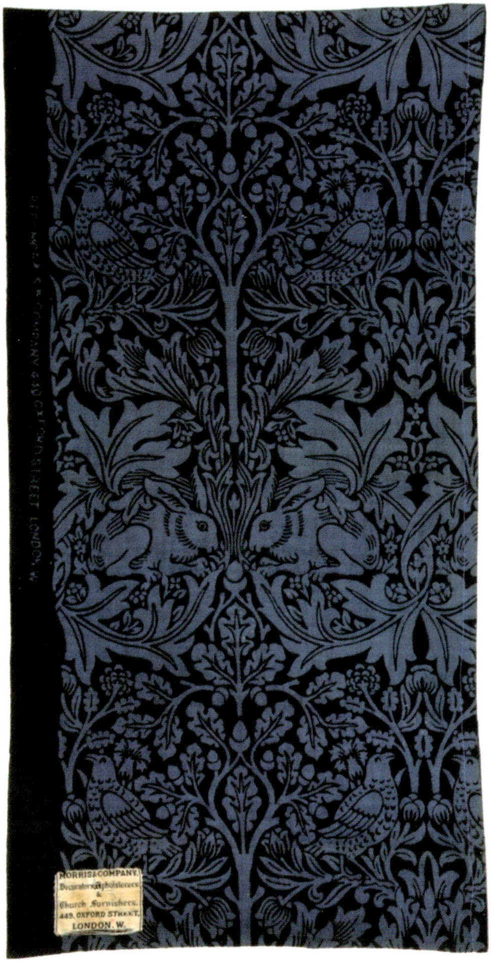

Fig.4. William Morris, *Brer Rabbit* furnishing fabric.
Indigo-discharged and block-printed cotton, 1882. Morris & Co.
William Morris Gallery, London.

Retelling Tales

The oral tradition of repeating stories, passing them from one generation to the next, led to them being altered gradually. Benjamin had an appropriate analogy for this process: he described how with each retelling 'traces of the storyteller cling to the story the way the handprints of the potter cling to the clay vessel'.[22] Morris was fascinated by 'the curious entanglement of the ages' that influenced a story and he admired the way in which medieval storytellers such as Chaucer reworked classical myths.[23] Morris also saw the classical world through medieval eyes. This vision was, according to his daughter May, 'not without some of the pleasant anachronisms that have endeared to us Flemish tapestry with their medieval representation of classical subject'.[24] This is a fitting comparison as Morris designed tapestries that, though depicting classical subjects, have a distinctly medieval feel. Together with Burne-Jones he designed a tapestry featuring Pomona, the Roman goddess of fruit trees. This design was also used as the basis for an embroidered panel carried out by the Royal School of Art Needlework in about 1885 (Fig.5). Pomona is shown against a background of scrolling acanthus leaves and flowers that recalls the verdure tapestries from 16th-century France and Flanders rather than classical art.[25]

Morris and Burne-Jones often returned to a favourite story, altering it with each retelling in order to suit a different material. *The Romance of the Rose*, for example, was the basis for an embroidered frieze in the mid 1870s and included in their elaborately illustrated edition of *The Works of Geoffrey Chaucer*, printed in 1896 by their private press. The interpretations of the story are subtly different. For the first panel of the embroidered frieze (Fig.1), Burne-Jones shows the dreamer gazing

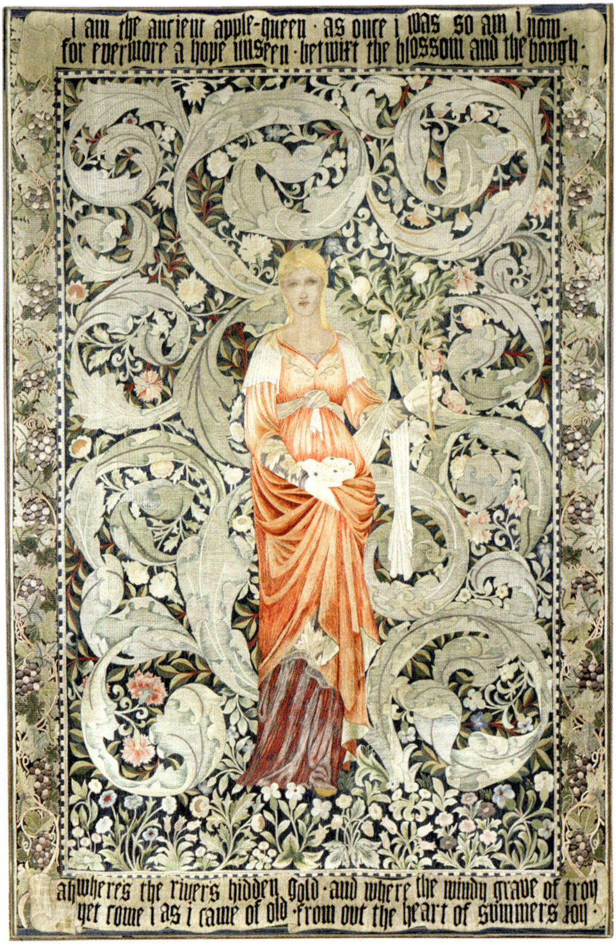

Fig.5. William Morris and Edward Burne-Jones, *Pomona* embroidered wall hanging.
Linen embroidered with floss silks, c.1885. Embroidered by The Royal School of Art Needlework.
Private Collection/The Bridgeman Art Library

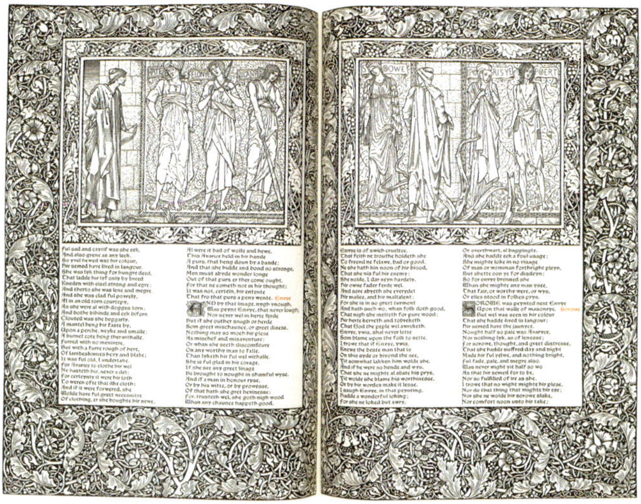

Fig.6. William Morris and Edward Burne-Jones, illustration for 'The Romance of the Rose' from *The Works of Geoffrey Chaucer*. Wood engraving on paper, 1896. Kelmscott Press. Senate House Library, University of London.

at a stone wall which is decorated with a series of niches containing statues. The statues are allegories of the vices such as hate, hypocrisy and poverty, their names written in gold on their plinths. The colour and direction of the embroidered stitches has produced the effect of light and shade and has given the figures a sculptural appearance. When illustrating the *Chaucer*, Burne-Jones found this scene difficult to interpret. He wrote, 'I wish Chaucer would once for all make up his unrivalled and precious mind whether he is talking of a picture or a statue'.[26] In his wood engraving (Fig.6) the allegories of the vices are shown not as a painting or a sculpture but as an embroidered or woven wall hanging. These wall hangings provide a link to the earlier embroidered frieze but also demonstrate the variety of ways in which a story can be depicted. For Morris, the handing down of stories was similar to the handing down of pattern motifs. He believed that 'No pattern should be without some sort of meaning. True it is that meaning may have come down to us traditionally, and not be our invention, yet we must at heart understand it, or we can neither receive it, nor hand it down to our successors'.[27] Patterns, like stories, could evoke both collective and personal memories. Textile and wallpaper designs, such as those that incorporate the acanthus leaf motif (Fig.7), draw upon a collective tradition. Morris stated that, 'No form of ornament has gone so far, or lasted so long as this; it has been infinitely varied'.[28] This was a motif that, like a folktale or legend, had been passed down through the generations and altered in the process of retelling. Other patterns had a more personal significance. The design *Medway* (Fig.8), with its undulating, meandering lines, was part of a series of textiles designed in the 1880s that recall, both through their structures and their titles, the tributaries of the Thames. This was a river with which Morris felt a deep personal connection – a river where he went sailing and fishing and a river which he wanted both to use and protect.[29]

The audience or viewer was as important as the storyteller or designer to creation of meaning. The continuation of the storytelling tradition relied, according to Benjamin, on there being a receptive community of listeners ready to commit the story to memory.[30] May Morris wrote about those 'lovers of Morris's art who have brought it into their own homes'. She evoked the experience of living with these patterned textiles and wallpapers and described how, 'Both to the real child and the child in the grown-up there is a story at the back of those decorated walls'. This decorated wall, 'as part of the background of childhood or of young married days' was invested with the house owner's personal memories.[31] Wallpaper patterns had become part of the everyday lives of a middle class public in contrast to the more expensive embroidered and woven hangings that had a very exclusive audience. It was, for instance, the owner of *The Romance of the Rose* frieze, Sir Isaac Lowthian Bell, who felt the force of Morris's angry proclamation that he spent his life in 'ministering to the swinish

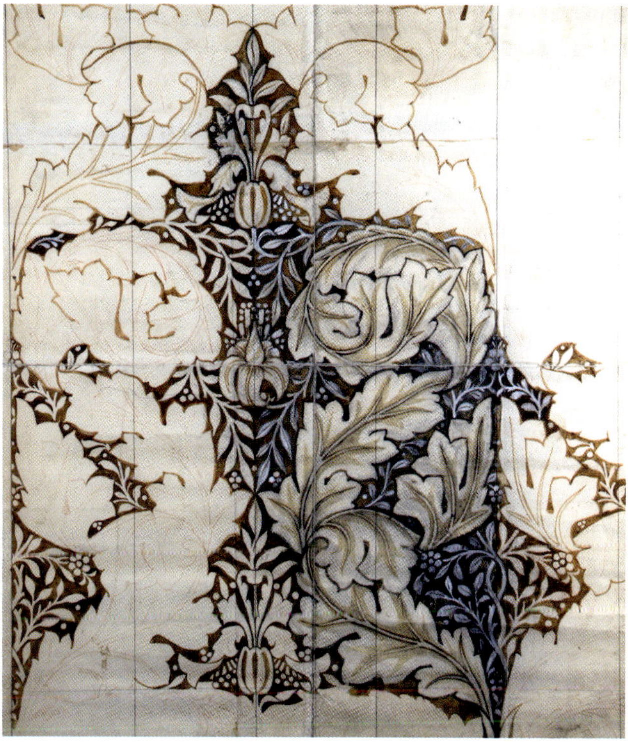

Fig.7. William Morris, design for *Acanthus* furnishing fabric.
Pencil and watercolour on paper, 1879. William Morris Gallery, London.

luxury of the rich'.[32] May lamented that 'great men' no longer ordered storied hangings for state halls and believed that the proper place for tapestries was in a fine public building: 'If these things were more in people's eyes they would grow to understand them'.[33]

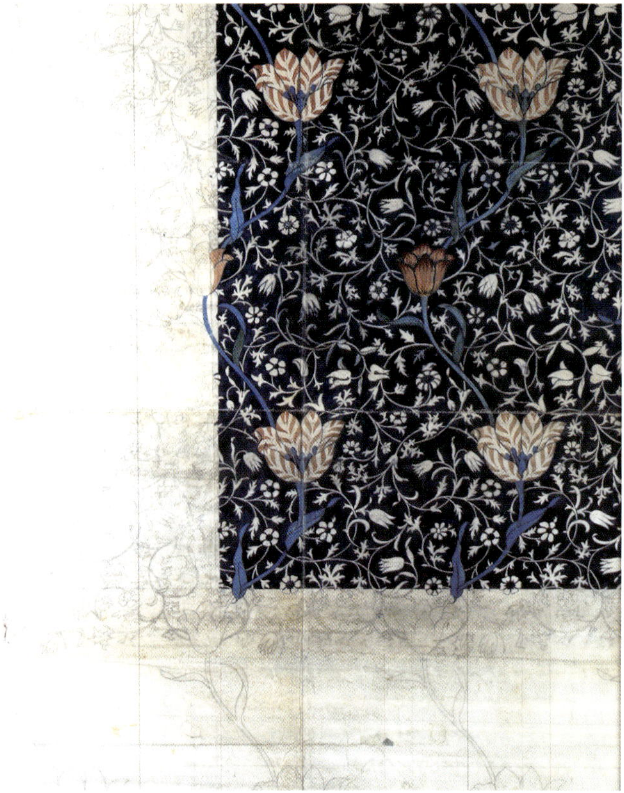

Fig.8. William Morris, design for *Medway* furnishing fabric.
Pencil and watercolour on paper, 1885. William Morris Gallery, London.

The Writing on the Wall

The communal act of sharing a story could still be achieved by looking at ancient buildings. The stones of Gothic churches and cathedrals could give a voice once again to their medieval builders who were otherwise 'voiceless for ever'.[34] This was an experience that Morris fought hard to preserve. As one of the founders of The Society for the Protection of Ancient Buildings, he campaigned to save the weathered and time-worn surface of ancient buildings from the hands of the restorer.[35] Morris believed that the textured surface of a wall, even without decoration, had the power to tell a tale and trigger memories. A story could be accessed not just by reading or looking but through touch. The importance of touch is conveyed in his story *News from Nowhere* when the character Ellen 'laid her shapely sun browned hand and arm on the lichened wall as if to embrace it' and unleashed thoughts of the earth 'and all things that deal with it, and all that grows out of it'.[36] In Burne-Jones's printed illustration of *The Romance of the Rose* (Fig.6), the dreamer not only looks at the decorated wall; he reaches out with his hand and touches it.

Morris battled, unsuccessfully, with the restoration architect John Loughborough Pearson over the appearance of a wall. Pearson had been given the task of preserving the surface of the masonry on the west side of Westminster Hall that was patterned with the marks of Romanesque builders. He proposed a two-storey 'cloister' which would 'recover the aspect which it presented in Richard II's time'.[37] Morris claimed that this restoration was based on conjecture and would therefore falsify the history of the building. He insisted that an inscription would be necessary stating, 'This building was built in such-and-such a year of the reign of Queen Victoria, and was done by such-and-such a gentleman, and it pretends to be old, and is not'.[38] Morris believed that the structure should be simple and obviously modern. A blank wall was always preferable to inappropriate decorations. 'After all a stone wall is a very good thing...A piece of architecture may be ugly; a stone wall cannot be'.[39]

In the exhibition *William Morris: Story, Memory, Myth*, Morris is reunited with his architectural rival. His designs for textiles, stained glass panels, ceramic tiles and wallpapers are displayed within Two Temple Place, a house designed by John Loughborough Pearson. Morris would not have approved of the money which William Waldorf Astor, the original owner, lavished on the building. However, he would have sympathised with Astor's request to have a house 'which would personify literature'.[40] Through the efforts of Pearson and his craftsmen, Two Temple Place was decorated with scenes and characters from literature. Beneath the roof of The Great Hall are twelve carved and gilded figures from Sir Walter Scott's *Ivanhoe*; its mahogany door has nine decorative panels in silver-gilt depicting heroines of Arthurian legend while the oak frieze above the staircase depicts scenes from Shakespeare. These were the same stories which Morris read as a child, in his student days at Oxford, and throughout his adult life. Although Two Temple Place was a private house rather than a state hall, Astor also wanted a noble and splendid building clad with stories. His rooms are now inhabited by the art and imagination of the gifted storyteller, William Morris.

Dr Esmé Whittaker, 2011

[1] William Morris, 'Textile Fabrics: A Lecture Delivered at the International Health Exhibition' (1884), in May Morris (ed.) *The Collected Works of William Morris*, 24 vols. (London: Longmans, Green & Co., 1910-15), xxii. 293-4.

[2] John Edmonds, *Chaucer's Other Works in Modern English Prose* (Morrisville: Lulu Enterprises, 2006), 427.

[3] William Morris, 'The Arts and Crafts of To-day' (1889), in May Morris (ed.) *The Collected Works*, xxii. 360.

[4] William Morris, 'Gothic Architecture' (1889), in Chris Miele (ed.), *William Morris on Architecture* (Sheffield: Sheffield Academic Press, 1996), 151.

[5] Walter Benjamin, 'The Storyteller', in Hannah Arendt (ed.) and Harry Zohn (trans.), *Illuminations* (London: Collins & Co., 1973), 85. For a full analysis of this text see Esther Leslie, 'Walter Benjamin: Traces of Craft', *Journal of Design History*, 11/1 (1998), 5-13.

[6] 'Master Printer Morris: A Visit to the Kelmscott Press', *Daily Chronicle*, 22 Feb. 1893, 3, in Tony Pinkney (ed.), *We Met Morris: Interviews with William Morris* (Reading: Spire Books, 2005). In his introduction, Pinkey describes Morris's 'hybrid identity'.

[7] William Morris quoted in J. W. Mackail, *The Life of William Morris*, 2 vols. (London: Longmans, Green, and Co., 1899; repr. New York: Dover Publications, 1995), i. 186.

[8] William Morris, *Poems by the Way* (London: Kelmscott Press, 1891).

[9] William Morris, 'Some Hints on Pattern-Designing' (1881), in May Morris (ed.) *The Collected Works*, xxii. 194.

[10] Ovid, *Metamorphoses*, trans. and ed. Charles Martin (New York: W. W. Norton & Company, 2010), 389-393.

[11] *The Earthly Paradise* was published in three volumes between 1868 and 1870 (London: F.S. Ellis).

[12] Benjamin, 'The Storyteller', 85.

[13] Ibid. 84.

[14] Christine Poulson, *The Quest for the Grail: Arthurian Legend in British Art 1840-1920* (Manchester: Manchester University Press, 1999), 7.

[15] H. E. Wroot, 'Pre-Raphaelite Windows at Bradford', *Studio*, 72 (Nov. 1917), 70.

[16] William Morris, 'Glass, Painted or Stained' (1890), Christine Poulson (ed.), *William Morris on Art and Design* (Sheffield: Sheffield Academic Press, 1996), 48.

[17] William Morris, *The Collected Letters of William Morris*, ed. Norman Kelvin, 3 vols. (Princeton: Princeton University Press, 1984-96), i. 181.

[18] Joel Chandler Harris, *Uncle Remus His Songs and His Sayings*, ed. and with an introduction by Robert Hemenway (London: Penguin Books, 1982), 29.

[19] Fiona MacCarthy, *William Morris: A Life for Our Time* (London: Faber and Faber, 2010), 548.

[20] May Morris, *William Morris: Artist, Writer, Socialist*, 2 vols. (Oxford, Basil Blackwell, 1936), i. 44.

[21] Ibid.

[22] Benjamin, 'The Storyteller', 92.

[23] May Morris, *William Morris*, 475.

[24] Ibid. 413.

[25] Linda Parry, *William Morris Textiles* (London: Weidenfeld and Nicolson, 1983), 108.

[26] Edward Burne-Jones quoted in Georgiana Burne-Jones, *Memorials of Edward Burne-Jones*, 2 vols. (London: MacMillan, 1904), ii. 217.

[27] William Morris, 'Making the Best of it' (1879) in May Morris (ed.) *The Collected Works*, xxii. 111. For further discussion of the relationship between storytelling and pattern design see Isolde Karen Herbert, 'The "Sympathetic Translation" of Patterns: William Morris as Singer, Scribe, and Printer', *Journal of William Morris Studies*, 13/4 (2000), 21-9.

[28] William Morris, 'The History of Pattern-Designing: A Lecture Delivered in Support of The Society for the Protection of Ancient Buildings' (1882), in May Morris (ed.) *The Collected Works*, xxii. 220.

[29] For a full exploration of Morris's relationship with the river see Caroline Arscott, *William Morris & Edward Burne-Jones: Interlacings* (New Haven: Yale University Press, 2008), 177-201.

[30] Benjamin, 'The Storyteller', 91.

[31] May Morris, *William Morris*, 34-5.

[32] Recorded by William Richard Lethaby, *Philip Webb and his Work* (London: Oxford University Press, 1935), 94-5.

[33] May Morris, *William Morris*, 54.

[34] William Morris, 'The Churches of North France, No. 1, Shadows of Amiens' (1856), in Miele (ed.), *William Morris on Architecture*, 11.

[35] William Morris, 'Architecture and History: A Paper Read Before The Society for the Protection of Ancient Buildings' (1884), in May Morris (ed.) *The Collected Works*, xxii. 296.

[36] William Morris, *News From Nowhere* (1890), in Poulson (ed.), *William Morris on Art and Design*, 137.

[37] Pearson's report for the Office of Works, quoted in Chris Miele, 'The Battle for Westminster Hall', *Architectural History*, 41 (1998), 230.

[38] *Report from the Select Committee on Westminster Hall Restoration; Together with the Proceedings of the Committee, Minutes of Evidence, and Appendix* (London: Henry Hansard and Son, 1885), 91.

[39] Ibid. 90.

[40] J. R. Willis Alexander, *Incorporated Accountants' Hall: Its History and Architecture* (London: The Society of Incorporated Accountants and Auditors, 1935), 16-9.

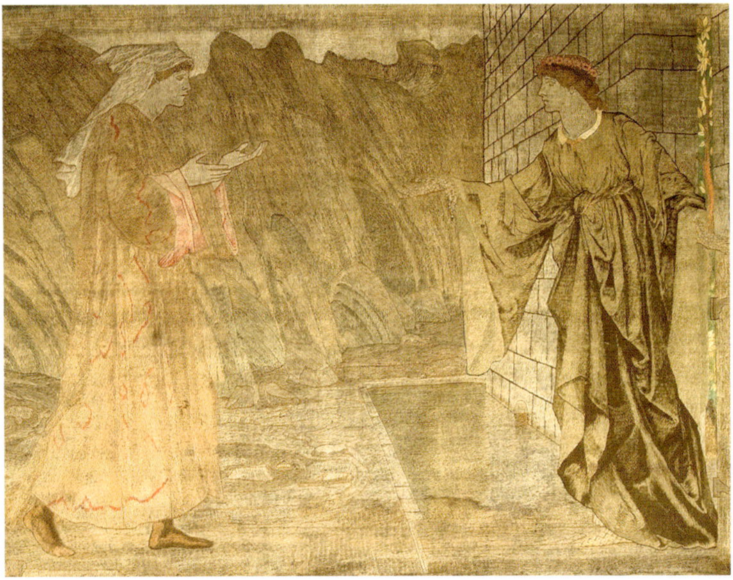

Edward Burne-Jones and William Morris, 'The Pilgrim Greeted by Idleness at the Gate of the Garden' from *The Romance of the Rose* embroidered frieze.
Linen embroidered with silks, wools and gold thread, 1874-82.
Embroidered by Margaret Bell and her daughter Florence.
William Morris Gallery, London.

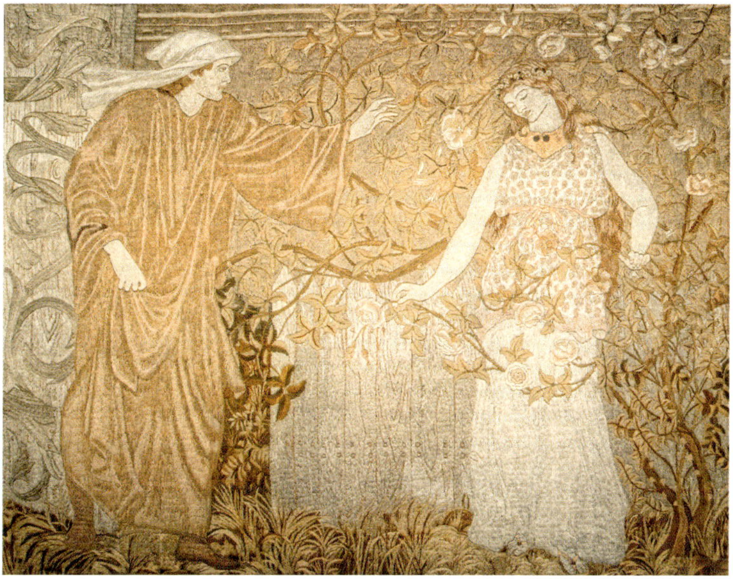

Edward Burne-Jones and William Morris, 'The Pilgrim at the Heart of the Rose' from *The Romance of the Rose* embroidered frieze.
Linen embroidered with silks, wools and gold thread, 1874-82.
Embroidered by Margaret Bell and her daughter Florence.
William Morris Gallery, London.

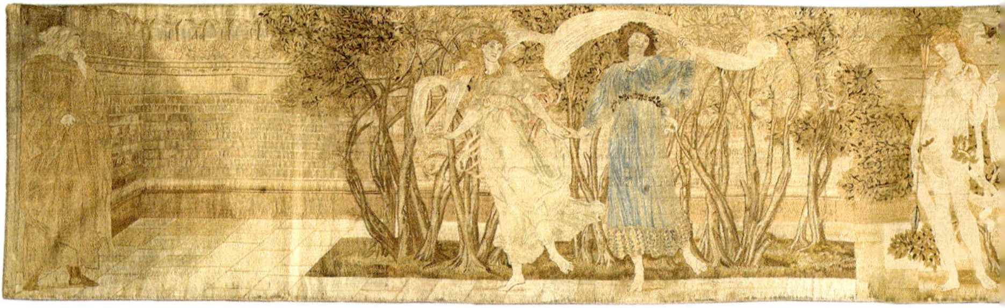

Edward Burne-Jones and William Morris, 'The Pilgrim in the Garden of Idleness' from *The Romance of the Rose* embroidered frieze. Linen embroidered with silks, wools and gold thread, 1874-82. Embroidered by Margaret Bell and her daughter Florence. William Morris Gallery, London.

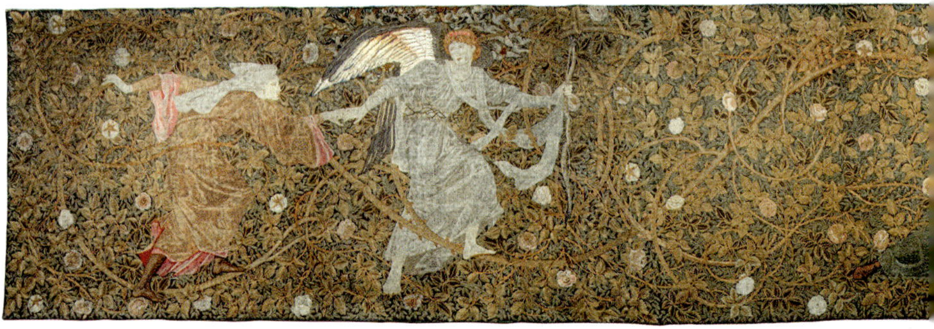

Edward Burne-Jones and William Morris, 'Love Leading the Pilgrim Through the Briars' from *The Romance of the Rose* embroidered frieze. Linen embroidered with silks, wools and gold thread, 1874-82. Embroidered by Margaret Bell and her daughter Florence. William Morris Gallery, London.

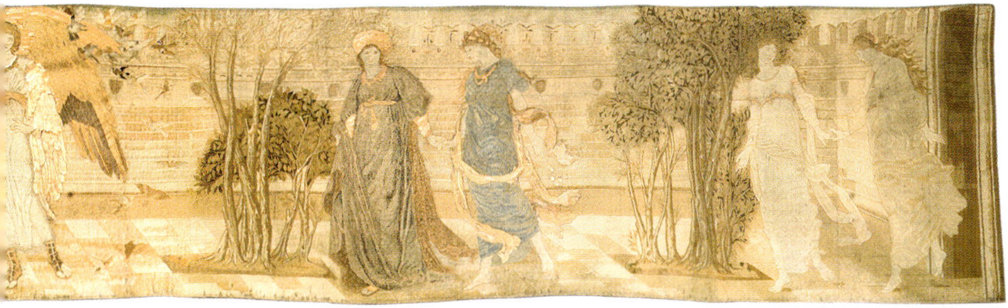

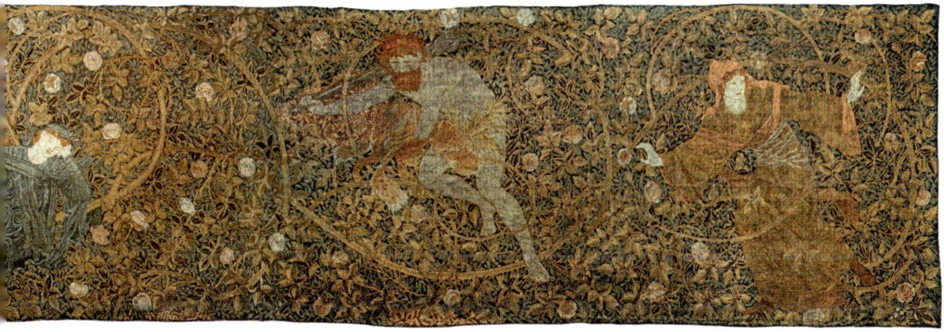

The Romance of the Rose

A medieval French poem styled as an allegorical dream vision. Guillaume de Lorris, who was the author of the first 4000 lines of the poem, declared that his intention was to expound the 'whole art of love'. He left the work unfinished when he died in about 1230. It was completed some 40 years later by Jean de Meun. In the 14th century Geoffrey Chaucer is said to have translated the first part of the work into Middle English as *The Romaunt of the Rose.*

The earlier part of the poem describes the Lover's quest for the Rose (which symbolises his beloved). Guillaume relates this story as if it were a dream, through the voice of the Lover.

In the dream, the Lover finds a walled garden, belonging to a nobleman called Deduit (meaning pleasure). He is invited to enter by a lady, Idleness, and is met by the dancing figures of the Virtues including Generosity of Spirit, Joy, Beauty and Kindness.

As he wanders through the garden he pauses by the Fountain of Narcissus. When he sees a vision of a rose in the water, the god of Love shoots him with several arrows and he is forever enamoured of this flower. He sets out to pluck the rose (win over his love), and in this he is tutored in the art of courtship by the winged god of Love. He is led by the god through a thicket of briar roses within which are allegories of the Vices he will encounter in his quest – Shame, Danger and Fear amongst others. The Lover experiences a journey filled with hope and despair, but although he eventually manages to kiss the rose his efforts prove futile after Jealousy imprisons the rose within a fortress.

In the latter part of the poem Jean de Meun's focus moves beyond that of courtly love and his interests are altogether wider and more scholarly. The allegorical figure of Reason is given a more prominent role, with Nature and Genius also appearing to give lengthy advice to the Lover. After gaining admittance to the fortress with the help of False Appearance and Forced Abstinence, the Lover finally succeeds in plucking the rose and consummating his love.

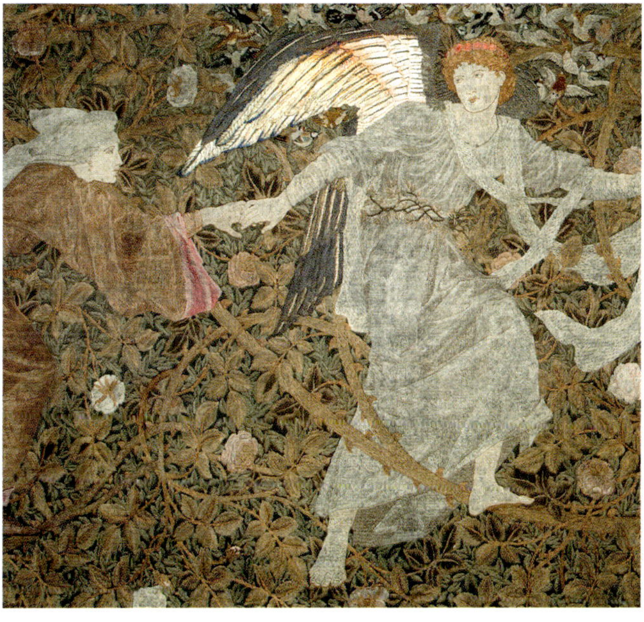

Detail from Edward Burne-Jones and William Morris, 'Love Leading the Pilgrim Through the Briars' from *The Romance of the Rose* embroidered frieze. Linen embroidered with silks, wools and gold thread, 1874-82. Embroidered by Margaret Bell and her daughter Florence. William Morris Gallery, London.

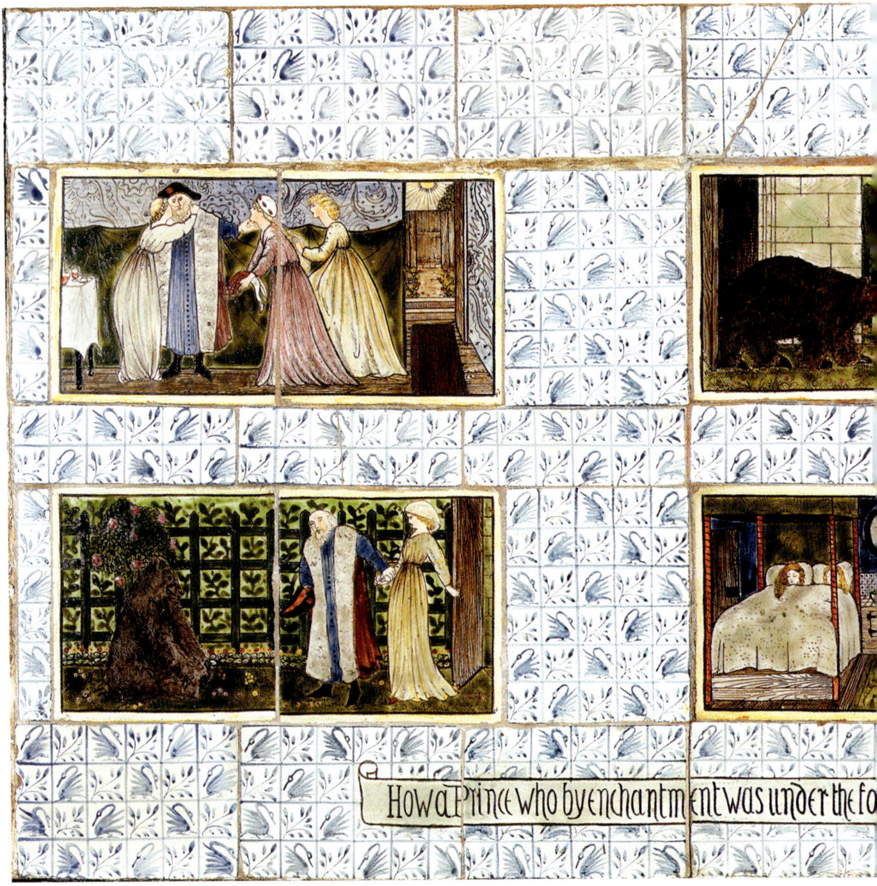

Edward Burne-Jones and William Morris, *Beauty and the Beast* tile panel with *Swan* border tiles.
Hand-painted on tin-glazed earthenware Dutch blanks, 1862.
Morris, Marshall, Faulkner & Co., painted by Lucy Faulkner.
William Morris Gallery, London.

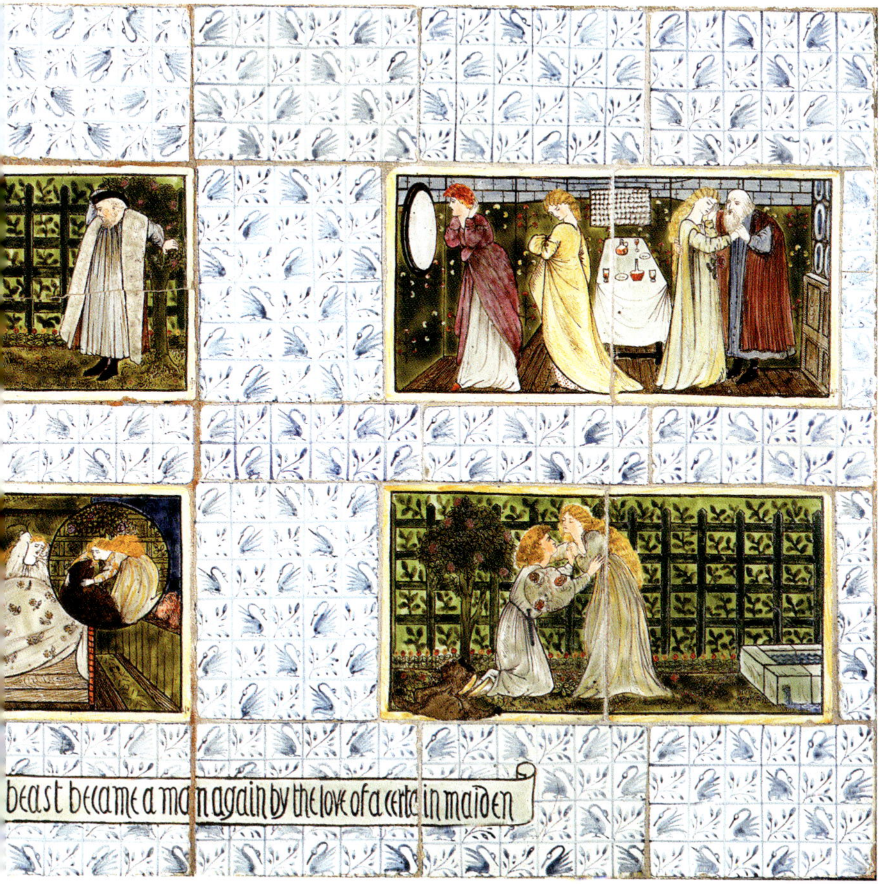
beast became a man again by the love of a certain maiden

Beauty and the Beast

A traditional fairy-tale of French origin, (the most well known version being that of Jeanne-Marie Le Prince de Beaumont) first published in 1756.

A wealthy merchant has three daughters, the most beautiful of whom is named Belle. The family having lost its wealth in a tempest at sea have retired to a small farmhouse, where the daughters are required to work. After some time the merchant receives a letter advising him to travel to the port where one of his ships is now docked, having escaped the storm. His two elder daughters, thinking that his fortune has now been restored demand that he bring them back jewels and fine robes. Belle, who is pure in heart, asks merely for a rose, as none will grow in their garden. The merchant sets out, but his journey is to prove fruitless for no cargo of any worth awaits him.

Upon his return the merchant becomes lost in a forest and shelters in a magnificent palace where he spends the night. In the morning, as he is about to leave he passes a rose garden and remembering Belle's request picks the loveliest rose he can find. Upon doing this he is confronted by a Beast who accuses him of stealing his most prized possession. The Beast threatens to take his life, only relenting after the merchant has agreed to return to the palace with Belle.

The merchant is then duly sent on his way laden down with jewels and fine clothes. At home he tries to keep the promise he has made to the Beast secret, but Belle manages to prise the truth from him. She willingly travels to the palace, knowing that this will save her father from danger. The Beast receives her graciously and she lives a life of great comfort. He tends to her every need and having fallen under her spell requests her hand in marriage every night. After each refusal she dreams of a handsome prince who pleads with her to re-consider his offer, but still she resists.

Eventually Belle becomes homesick and pleads with the Beast to allow her to visit her family. He agrees to her leaving for one week only, under the condition that she takes a ring with her, which when placed upon a table beside her bed will allow her to return to the palace in an instant.

When her sisters see Belle dressed in all her finery and more beautiful than ever they are overcome with jealousy. So at the end of the week they beg her to stay, in the hope that the Beast will be so enraged with Belle for breaking her promise that he will eat her alive.

Belle is so moved by her sister's seemingly genuine show of affection that she relents. But a few nights later she dreams that the Beast is lying in the palace gardens, weak and heartbroken. Upon awakening she places the ring on her bedside table and is at once back at the palace. There she finds the Beast as he has appeared in her dream. She weeps over him, declaring her love and in so doing breaks the spell that has been cast over him. The Beast is transformed back into a handsome prince. The two of them are married... and of course they live happily ever after.

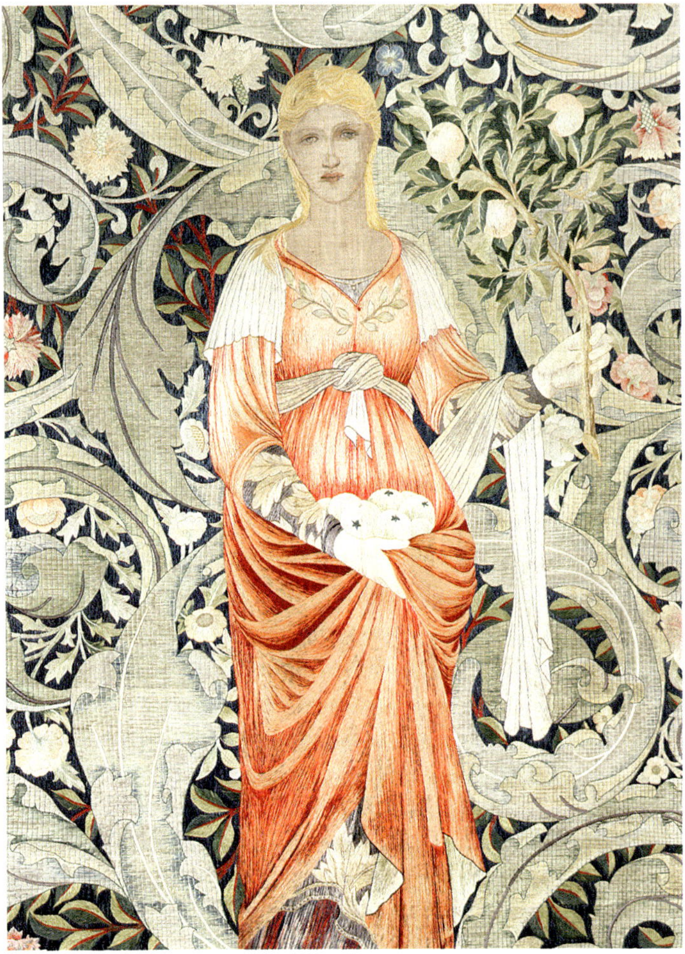

Detail of William Morris and Edward Burne-Jones, *Pomona* embroidered wall hanging.
Linen embroidered with floss silks, c.1885. Embroidered by The Royal School of Art Needlework.
Private Collection/The Bridgeman Art Library

Pomona

Pomona was the Roman goddess of fruits and orchards, her name being derived from the Latin word pomum for 'fruit'.

It was said that both Silvanus (a Roman spirit of the woods and fields) and Picus (King of Ausonia) sought her favours but to no avail.

However, in Ovid's *Metamorphoses* she falls in love with Vertumnus (the Roman god of seasons and change) in a story of seduction and deception.

Pomona, at the start of the tale has decided to shun the company of men and has withdrawn into her beloved orchard. However, by using his ability to transform at will, Vertumnus is able to frequently gain admittance to this retreat and gaze upon her beauty. He disguises himself as a reaper of hay, apple picker, fisherman, but it is finally as an old woman that he is able to talk to her at length.

In this disguise he then uses a story (that of Iphis and Anaxarete) warning of the dangers involved in rejecting another's advances, in order to seduce her. Having begged her to 'put aside reluctant pride and yield to your lover' he then reveals himself in his true form, as a god, and Pomona is captivated by him.

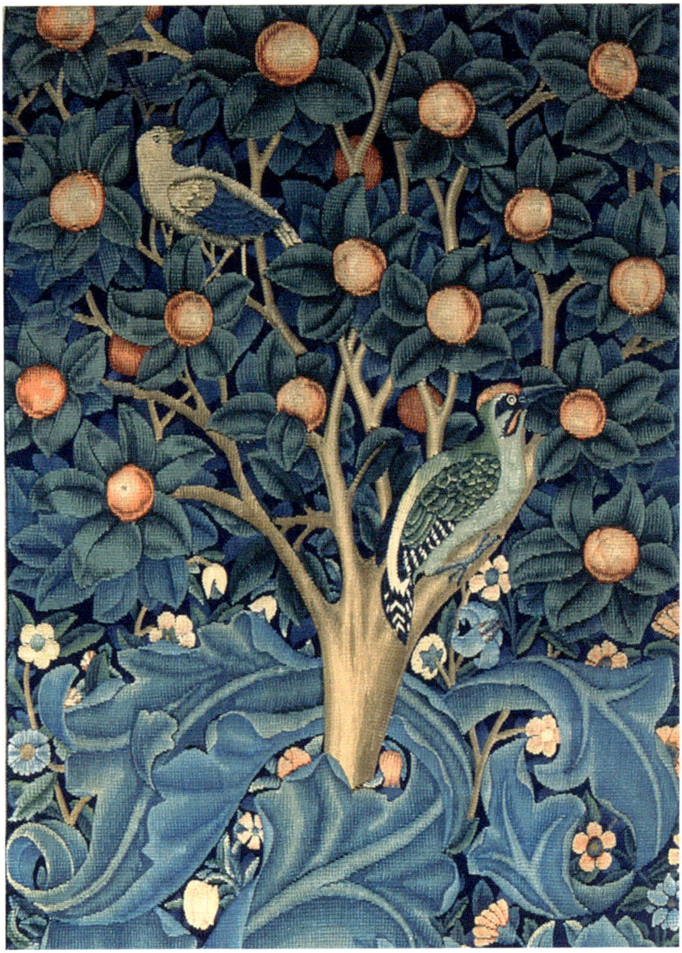

Detail of William Morris, *The Woodpecker* tapestry.
Woven wool and silk on a cotton warp, 1885. Morris & Co.
William Morris Gallery, London.

Picus

In Roman mythology Picus was an early king of Ausonia. He was renowned for his horsemanship and his skill in augury, in which he was able to interpret the will of the Gods through studying the behaviour of birds and the appearance of entrails. As would befit a seer at the time, he was depicted as possessing a green woodpecker, the pre-eminent prophetic bird.

Later it would be claimed (most notably in Ovid's *Metamorphoses*) that the woodpecker was in fact Picus himself. He had been transformed into a bird by the enchantress Circe, in a fit of pique.

It was said that one day while out hunting for wild boar in the woods, Picus was met by Circe, who was at once overwhelmed by her passionate feelings for him. However, he was already devoted to his wife, the nymph Canens, who possessed a rare beauty and a voice that could make wild beasts gentle. His loyalty to her meant that he did not hesitate in rejecting Circe, despite her intense pleadings with him.

In anger at his rejection Circe cursed him and he was changed into a woodpecker and his companions into wild beasts. When Canens learnt of his fate, she wandered throughout the land in despair, eventually wasting away. Some versions have her vanishing into thin air, so that all that remained was a voice.

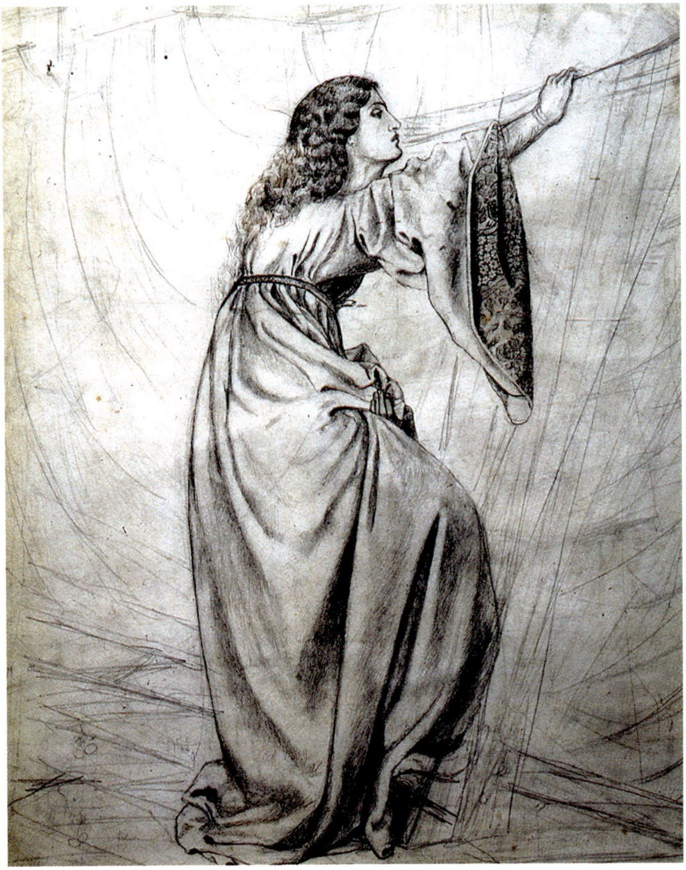

William Morris, Study of Jane Morris for a wall painting.
Pencil and ink on paper, c.1861.
William Morris Gallery, London.

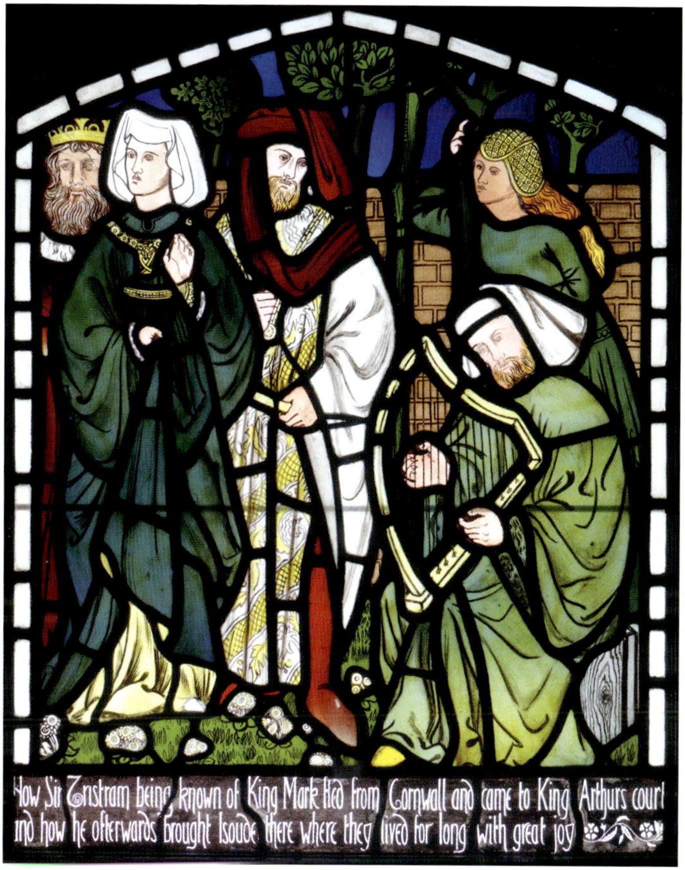

William Morris, 'Tristram and La Belle Isoude at Arthur's Court', from *The Story of Tristram and Isoude* series. Stained-glass panel, 1862. Morris, Marshall, Faulkner & Co. Bradford Museums and Galleries.

Tristram and Isoude

A tragic story of adulterous love between the Cornish knight Tristram (Tristan) and the Irish princess Isoude (Iseult, Isolde). This romance has a long and varied literary history, with the legend being recounted by Thomas of Britain and Beroul in the latter part of the twelfth century.

In about 1240 a markedly different interpretation of the story appeared with the *Prose Tristan*, which would provide the inspiration for the writings of Sir Thomas Malory who included a version of the story in his *Le Morte Darthur.*

Sir Tristram, under the advice of a wise woman travels to Ireland to be cured of his lingering war wounds. There he is tended upon by La Belle Isoude. When he returns to Cornwall he informs his uncle King Mark of the kind treatment he has received.

On hearing his account King Mark falls in love with La Belle Isoude and sends Tristram back to Ireland to woo her for him. Sir Tristram succeeds in his task and Isoude accepts King Mark's proposal of marriage.

However, on the return journey to Cornwall the two inadvertently drink a love potion (meant to ensure Isoude's happiness with King Mark) and they fall in love. But Isoude is already promised to King Mark and they are wed. Isoude and Tristram then spend the rest of their lives attempting to satisfy their desire for each other without revealing that desire to King Mark and the Cornish court.

After numerous trysts the lovers become estranged, and Tristram marries another Isoude de Blanche Mains (of the White Hands) although the marriage is never consummated. Their enforced separation causes them heartache – Tristram becomes mad and La Belle Isoude attempts suicide, only to be saved by King Mark.

Eventually they are reconciled and live together for some time at the court of King Arthur. However, their happiness is short lived, as King Mark kills an unarmed Tristram, as he is playing his harp for Isoude. She dies of a broken heart.

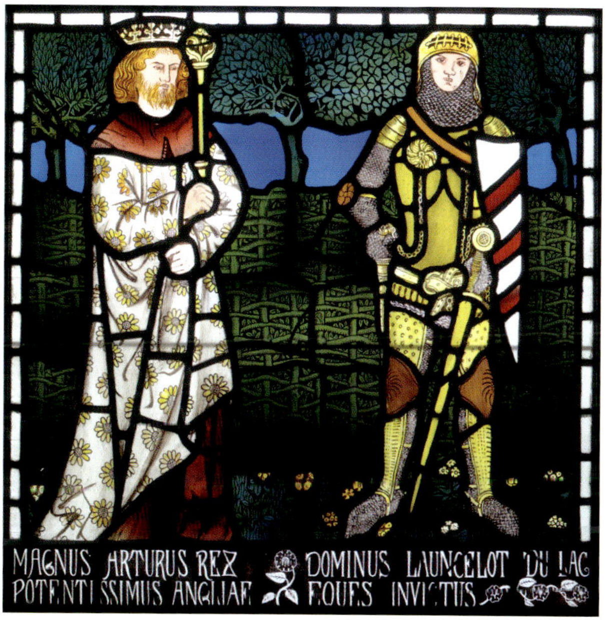

William Morris, 'King Arthur and Sir Launcelot', from *The Story of Tristram and Isoude* series. Stained-glass panel, 1862. Morris, Marshall, Faulkner & Co. Bradford Museums and Galleries.

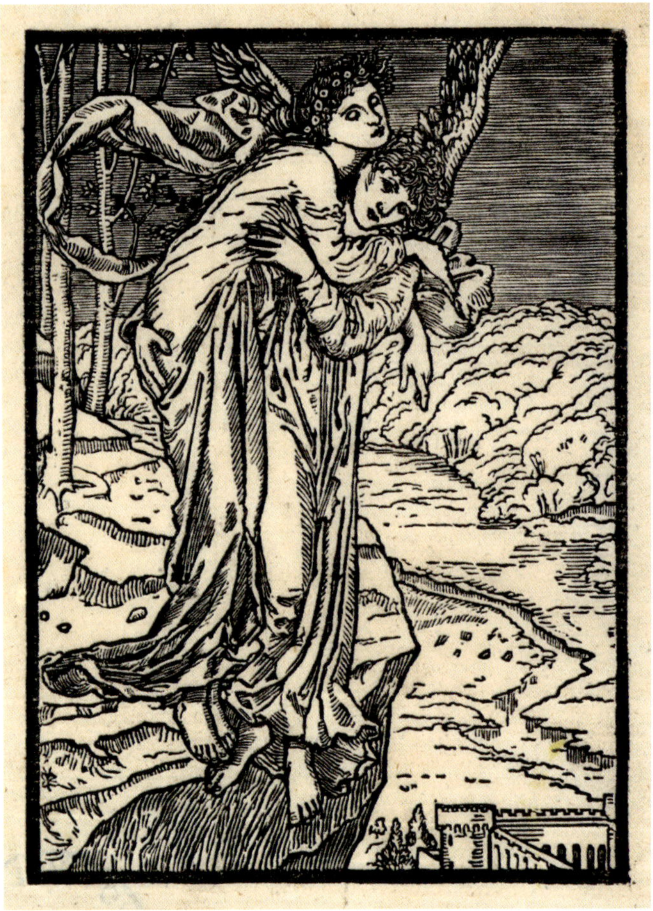

Edward Burne-Jones, *Zephyrus and Psyche* illustration for 'The Story of Cupid and Psyche' in *The Earthly Paradise* by William Morris. Wood engraving on paper, 1866-68. William Morris Gallery, London.

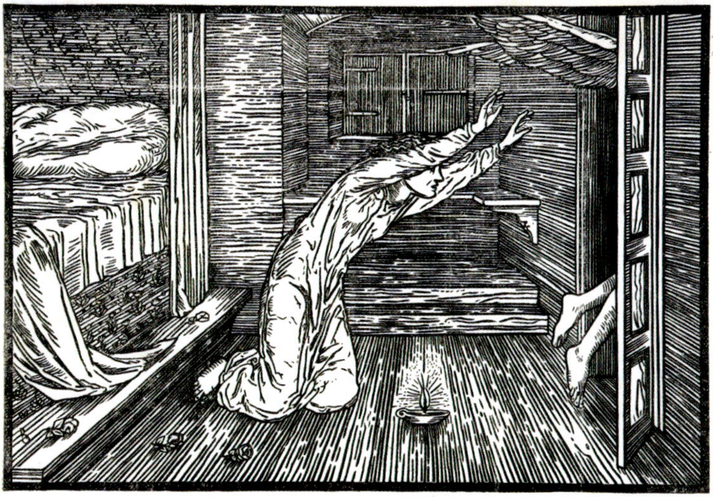

Edward Burne-Jones, *Cupid Going Away*, illustration for 'The Story of Cupid and Psyche' in *The Earthly Paradise* by William Morris. Wood engraving on paper, 1866-68. William Morris Gallery, London.

Cupid and Psyche

A legend that first appeared in Lucius Apuleius' novel *The Golden Ass*, written in the 2nd century AD.

The princess Psyche is so beautiful that Venus (the goddess of love and fertility) has become jealous. So she sends her son Cupid to aim one of his arrows at her while she is asleep – planning that when Psyche awakes she will instantly fall in love with the vile creature that Venus has cunningly placed before her. But distracted by her beauty Cupid accidentally scratches himself with the arrow instead and falls deeply in love with her.

Upon hearing of this turn of events Venus is enraged and curses Psyche, preventing her from finding a husband. In response a forlorn and lovesick Cupid vows not to fire any arrows until the curse has been lifted. And so for months no man or beast procreates and the earth becomes old. At this Venus is moved to ask Cupid to take up his bow and arrow again, and he agrees to do so in exchange for the love of Psyche.

During this time Psyche has not lacked admirers but is without a suitor. In despair her parents have consulted an oracle who has told them that she is destined to be married to a monster and instructs them to lead her to a nearby mountain top and abandon her to her fate. She is taken from there by Zephyrus (the god of the west wind) and carried to a magnificent palace, where she is waited upon by invisible servants and visited under nightfall by a lover, who eventually becomes her husband. This is Cupid, who has forbidden her from seeing him, until he considers that the time is right.

Psyche, while accustomed to life in the palace, grows homesick and persaudes her husband to allow her sisters to visit her. When they see her opulent surroundings they become jealous and convince her that she has married a monster who is fattening her up in order to devour her and their unborn child. They urge Psyche to light a lamp once her husband is asleep and see his true form. When she follows their advice she recognizes him as the god Cupid and overwhelmed by desire for him bends to kiss him. In so doing she tips the lamp over and a drop of oil falls upon his shoulder. He awakes and declaring that his trust in her is now gone, departs.

Psyche is heartbroken and spends the next few years wandering the land in search of Cupid. In desperation she turns to Venus and undertakes three seemingly impossible tasks in the hope of seeing her beloved once more.

For her final task she is to descend into the Underworld and bring back water from the fountain of youth, to restore the beauty that Venus has lost, whilst caring for her son Cupid. Psyche manages the perilous descent and in overcoming the obstacles and lures of the Underworld obtains the liquid in a vial which she places in a casket.

Upon reaching the world of the living Psyche is tempted to open the box and beautify herself with a drop of the potion, in the hope of tempting Cupid back to her side.

She opens the casket and poisonous fumes envelop her. Cupid appears by her side, closes the box and rouses her from her sleep with a kiss. Psyche and Cupid are united once more and Psyche is granted immortality.

Exhibition Object List

The object list is correct at the time of going to press.

Retelling Tales

Ford Madox Brown, study for *Chaucer at the Court of Edward III.*
Oil on board. 29.5 x 30.77 cm. About 1847-51.
William Morris Gallery, London.

William Morris and Edward Burne-Jones,
trial page for the 'Prologue', *The Works of Geoffrey Chaucer.*
Printed on vellum. 52 x 39 cm. 1896.
Kelmscott Press.
William Morris Gallery, London.

The Romance of the Rose

Edward Burne-Jones and William Morris,
The Romance of the Rose embroidered frieze.
Linen embroidered with silks, wools and gold thread. Five panels, 88 x 622 cm, 92 x 123 cm, 86.3 x 628.7 cm, 88 x 582 cm, 96.5 x 126 cm. 1874-82.
Embroidered by Margaret Bell and her daughter Florence.
William Morris Gallery, London.

William Morris and Edward Burne-Jones,
The Works of Geoffrey Chaucer.
Paper. 42.5 x 29.2 cm leaf. 1896.
Kelmscott Press.
William Morris Gallery, London.

William Morris and Edward Burne-Jones,
The Works of Geoffrey Chaucer.
Paper with buckram binding. 42.5 x 29.2 cm leaf. 1896.
Kelmscott Press; Facsimile by The Folio Society, 2008
Donated by The Folio Society, 2011

Edward Burne-Jones, study for the figure of *Fraunchise* for *The Romance of the Rose* embroidered frieze.
Pencil on paper. 25.4 x 18 cm. About 1874.
William Morris Gallery, London.

Edward Burne-Jones, *The Heart of the Rose.*
Charcoal and coloured chalks on paper. 84 x 130 cm. 1889.
William Morris Gallery, London.

William Morris, *Rose* wallpaper.
Block-printed on paper. 180 x 58 cm. 1877, reprinted about 1950.
Arthur Sanderson & Sons Ltd.
William Morris Gallery, London.

The Legend of Good Women

Edward Burne-Jones, *The God of Love and Alceste.*
Stained and painted glass. 63 x 74 cm. 1864.
Morris, Marshall, Faulkner & Co.
William Morris Gallery, London. Purchased with support from the MGC/V&A Purchase Grant Fund, the N.A.C.F., the Friends of the William Morris Gallery, NADFAS West Essex.

Edward Burne-Jones, design for *Thisbe* embroidered hanging.
Watercolour with bodycolour over black chalk on paper.
140 x 70 cm. 1862.
William Morris Gallery, London.

William Morris, *Acanthus* wallpaper. Block-printed on paper, 1875.
Jeffrey & Co. for Morris & Co.
William Morris Gallery, London.

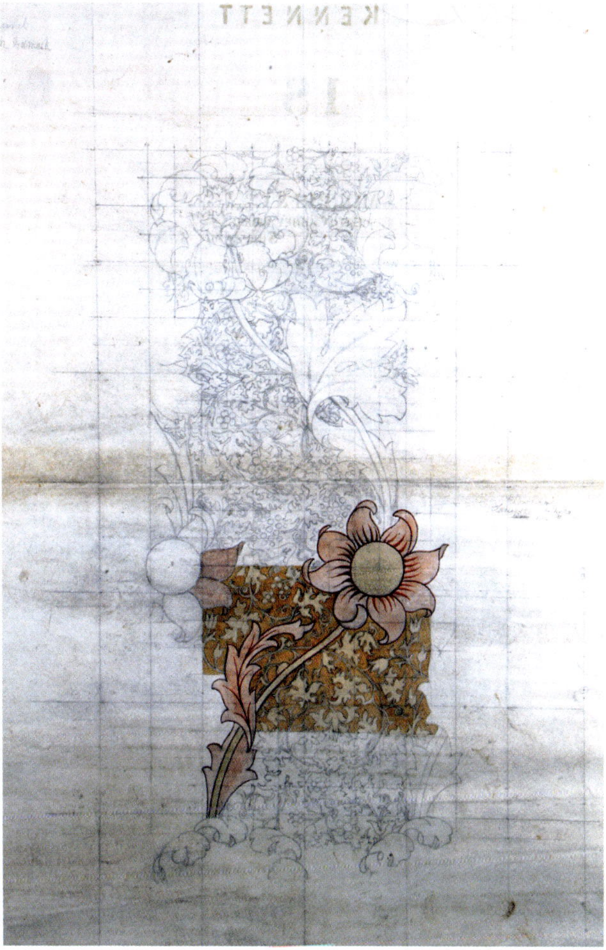

William Morris, design for *Kennet* furnishing fabric.
Pencil and watercolour on paper. 1883.
William Morris Gallary, London.

Edward Burne-Jones and William Morris, *Alceste* tile with surrounding tiles depicting a pomegranate tree.
Hand-painted on tin-glazed earthenware Dutch blanks.
26 x 13 cm Alceste tile. 1861-2.
Morris, Marshall, Faulkner & Co.
William Morris Gallery, London.

Memory & Motif

The River

William Morris, design for *Medway* furnishing fabric.
Pencil and watercolour on paper. 121 x 95 cm. 1885.
William Morris Gallery, London.

William Morris, *Medway* furnishing fabric.
Indigo-discharged and block-printed cotton. 77.5 x 65.5 cm. 1885.
Morris & Co.
William Morris Gallery, London.

William Morris, *Evenlode* furnishing fabric.
Indigo-discharged and block-printed cotton. 80 x 99 cm. 1883.
Morris & Co.
William Morris Gallery, London.

William Morris, design for *Kennet* furnishing fabric.
Pencil and watercolour on paper. 103.3 x 72.1 cm. 1883.
William Morris Gallery, London.
William Morris, *Kennet* furnishing fabric.
Woven silk. 70 x 80.5 cm. 1883.
Morris & Co.
William Morris Gallery, London.

The Acanthus Leaf

William Morris, design for *St. James's* wallpaper.
Pencil and watercolour on paper. 199 x 57.2 cm. 1881.
William Morris Gallery, London.

William Morris, *St. James's* wallpaper.
Block-printed on paper. 140 x 56.7 cm. 1881.
Jeffrey & Co. for Morris & Co.
William Morris Gallery, London.

William Morris, *Acanthus* wallpaper.
Block-printed on paper. 70.2 x 52 cm. 1875.
Jeffrey & Co. for Morris & Co.
William Morris Gallery, London.

William Morris, design for *Acanthus* furnishing fabric.
Pencil and watercolour on paper. 124 x 98 cm. 1879.
William Morris Gallery, London.

The Holy Tree

William Morris, design for *Peacock and Bird* carpet.
Pencil and sepia on paper. 77 x 78 cm. About 1885.
William Morris Gallery, London.

William Morris, working drawing (point paper) for
Dove and Rose furnishing fabric.
Watercolour on paper. 118 x 51.5 cm. 1879
William Morris Gallery, London.

William Morris, *Dove and Rose* furnishing fabric.
Hand-loom jacquard-woven silk and wool double cloth. 77 x 101.5 cm. 1879.
Alexander Morton & Co for Morris & Co., later manufactured by Morris & Co.
William Morris Gallery, London.

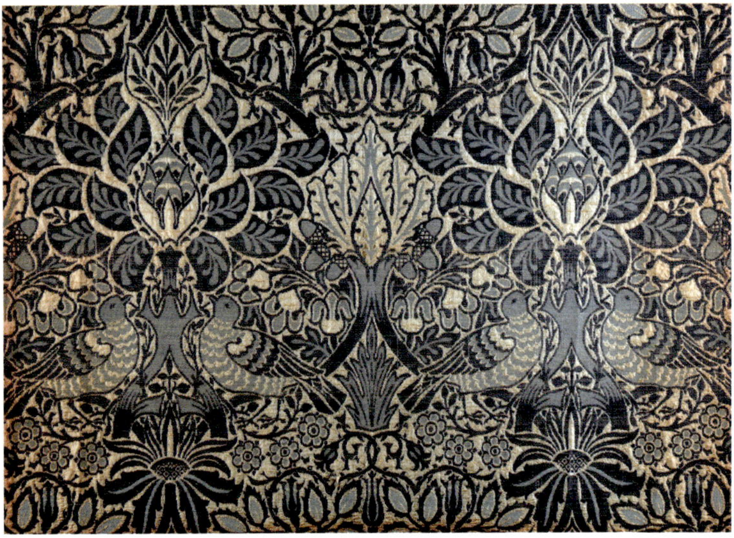

William Morris, *Dove and Rose* furnishing fabric.
Hand-loom jacquard-woven silk and wool double cloth, 1879. Morris & Co.
William Morris Gallery, London.

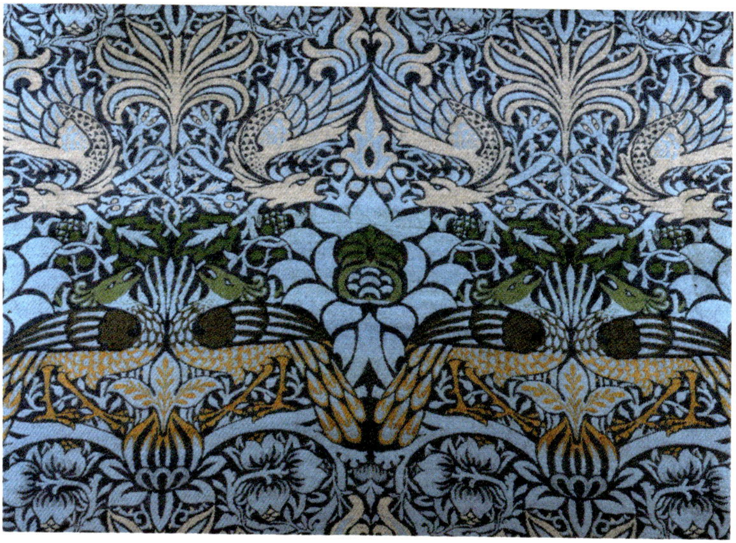

William Morris, *Peacock and Dragon* furnishing fabric.
Hand-loom jacquard-woven woollen twill, 1878. Morris & Co.
William Morris Gallery, London.

William Morris, design for *Bird and Palm Tree* furnishing fabric.
Pencil and ink on paper. 116 x 78 cm. Not put into production.
William Morris Gallery, London.

Fairytale & Folklore

William Morris and Edward Burne-Jones, design for *Mermaid* furnishing fabric or wallpaper.
Pencil, pen and watercolour on paper. 160 x 127 cm.
Not put into production.
William Morris Gallery, London.

William Morris, *Peacock and Dragon* furnishing fabric.
Hand-loom jacquard-woven woollen twill. 138 x 85 cm. 1878.
Morris & Co.
William Morris Gallery, London.

Edward Burne-Jones, *Cinderella* tiles.
Hand-painted on tin-glazed earthenware Dutch blanks.
15.24 x 15.24 cm each. About 1862.
Morris, Marshall, Faulkner & Co., painted by Kate or Lucy Faulkner. William Morris Gallery, London. Purchased with support from the V&A Purchase Grant Fund and the Friends of the William Morris Gallery.

William Morris, *Brer Rabbit* furnishing fabric.
Indigo-discharged and block-printed cotton. 73 x 99 cm. 1882.
Morris & Co.
William Morris Gallery, London.

William Morris, *Brer Rabbit* furnishing fabric.
Block-printed cotton. 177 x 95 cm. 1882.
Morris & Co.
William Morris Gallery, London.

Edward Burne-Jones and William Morris, *Beauty and the Beast* tile panel with *Swan* border tiles.
Hand-painted on tin-glazed earthenware Dutch blanks.
61 x 127 cm. 1862.
Morris, Marshall, Faulkner & Co., painted by Lucy Faulkner.
William Morris Gallery, London.

Exchanging Myths

William Morris, study of Jane Morris for a wall painting.
Pencil and ink on paper. 51 x 41 cm. About 1861.
William Morris Gallery, London.

May Morris, *June* embroidered frieze with inscription from William Morris's *The Earthly Paradise*.
Wools on linen. 91 x 302 cm. 1900.
William Morris Gallery, London.

William Morris and Edward Burne-Jones, *Pomona* embroidered wall hanging.
Linen embroidered with floss silks. 297.2 x 213.4 cm. About 1885.
Embroidered by The Royal School of Art Needlework.
Private Collection.

William Morris, *The Woodpecker* tapestry.
Woven wool and silk on a cotton warp. 307 x 156 cm. 1885.
Morris & Co.
William Morris Gallery, London.

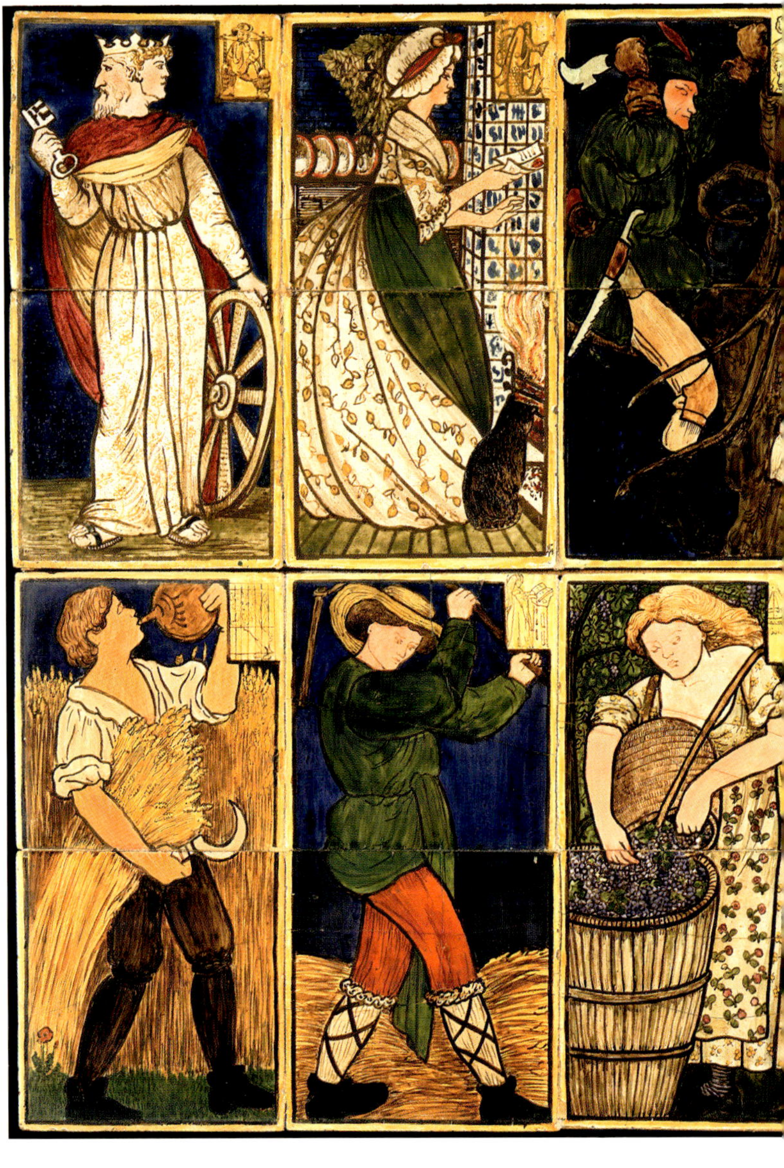

William Morris, Ford Madox Brown, Edward Burne-Jones, Dante Gabriel Rossetti and Philip Webb, *The Labours of the Months* tiles. Hand-painted on tin-glazed earthenware Dutch blanks, 1863. Painted by Lucy Faulkner for Morris, Marshall, Faulkner & Company.

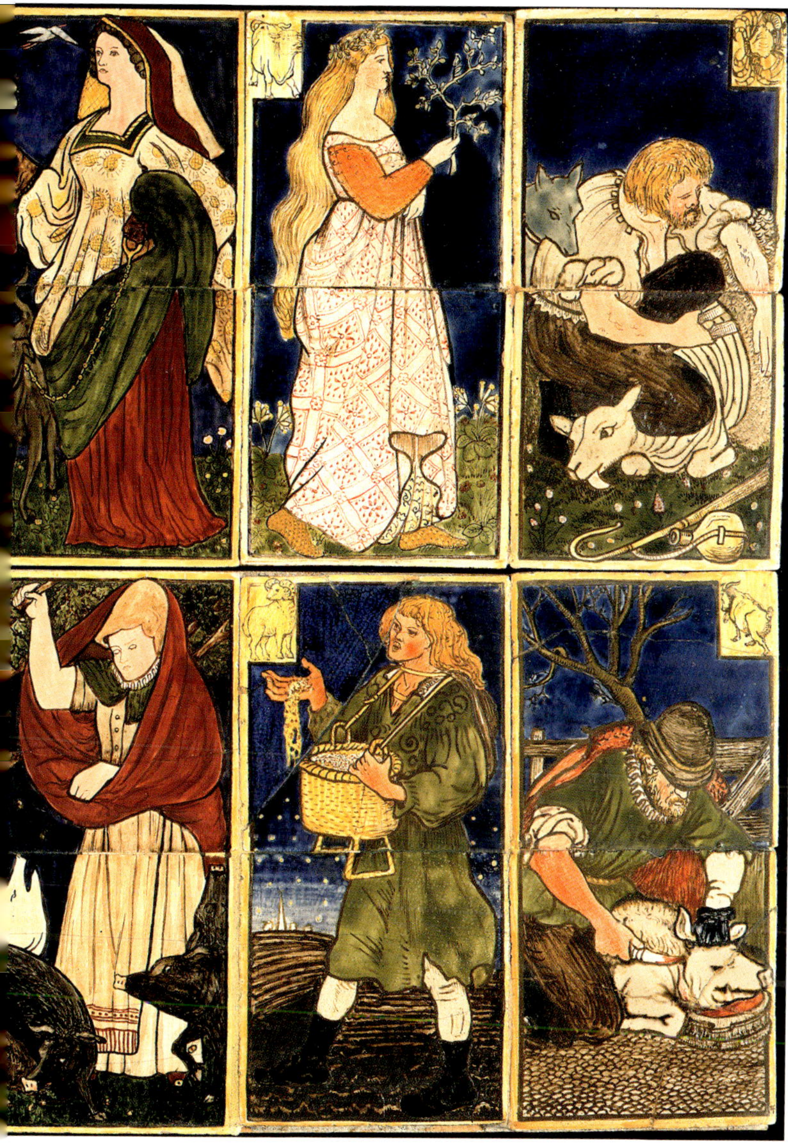

William Morris Gallery, London.
Purchased with support from the MGC/V&A Purchase Grant Fund,
the N.H.M.F., Friends of the William Morris Gallery and Walthamstow Historical Society.

Arthurian Legend

Edward Burne-Jones, cartoon for *The Summons* tapestry, Sir Launcelot and Sir Ector de Marys, from *The Holy Grail* series.
Watercolour, gouache and ink over photographic image on paper, laid down on canvas. 75 x 79 cm. 1890-1.
William Morris Gallery, London.

Edward Burne-Jones, cartoon for *The Summons* tapestry, Sir Palomydes and Sir Bors de Ganys, from *The Holy Grail* series.
Watercolour, gouache and ink over photographic image on paper, laid down on canvas. 207.5 x 85 cm. 1890-1.
William Morris Gallery, London.

Edward Burne-Jones, designs for *The Quest for the Sangreal* stained-glass panels.
Watercolour, ink, Chinese white, gold paint & graphite on paper, laid down on boards. 58.2 x 46 cm each. 1885-6.
William Morris Gallery, London.

William Morris, design for *King Arthur and Sir Launcelot* stained-glass panel from the *The Story of Tristram and Isoude* series.
Black and sepia washes and pencil on paper. 78 x 85.8 cm. 1862.
William Morris Gallery, London.

William Morris, *The Story of Tristram and Isoude.*
Stained glass panels. 68 x 60.5 cm, 77 x 61 cm, 71 x 71.5 cm, 71 x 71.5 cm. 1862.
Morris, Marshall, Faulkner & Co.
Bradford Museums and Galleries.

William Morris, *The Defence of Guenevere, and other Poems.*
Paper with vellum binding. 21 cm leaf. 1892.
Kelmscott Press.
William Morris Gallery, London.

Dante Gabriel Rossetti, *The Loving Cup.*
Watercolour on paper. 52.7 x 35.6 cm. 1867.
William Morris Gallery, London.

Edward Burne-Jones, *Saint George and the Dragon.*
Gouache on paper. 61.9 x 48.4 cm. 1868.
William Morris Gallery, London.

The Earthly Paradise

Edward Burne-Jones, illustrations for 'The Story of Cupid and Psyche' for an unrealised edition of *The Earthly Paradise* by William Morris. Wood engravings on paper. About 1866-8.
William Morris Gallery, London.

Edward Burne-Jones, *Cupid Leaving Psyche* wood block for an unrealised edition of *The Earthly Paradise* by William Morris.
Boxwood. 10.5 x 8 cm. About 1865.
Drawn on the block by William Morris, cut by Lucy Faulkner.
William Morris Gallery, London.

William Morris, *The Earthly Paradise.*
Wood engraving by Edward Burne-Jones. 19 x 13.5 cm leaf.
Fifth edition, 1870.
Published by F. S. Ellis.
William Morris Gallery, London.

William Morris, *The Earthly Paradise.*
Paper with vellum binding. 24 cm leaf. Vol. III, 1896.
Kelmscott Press.
William Morris Gallery, London.

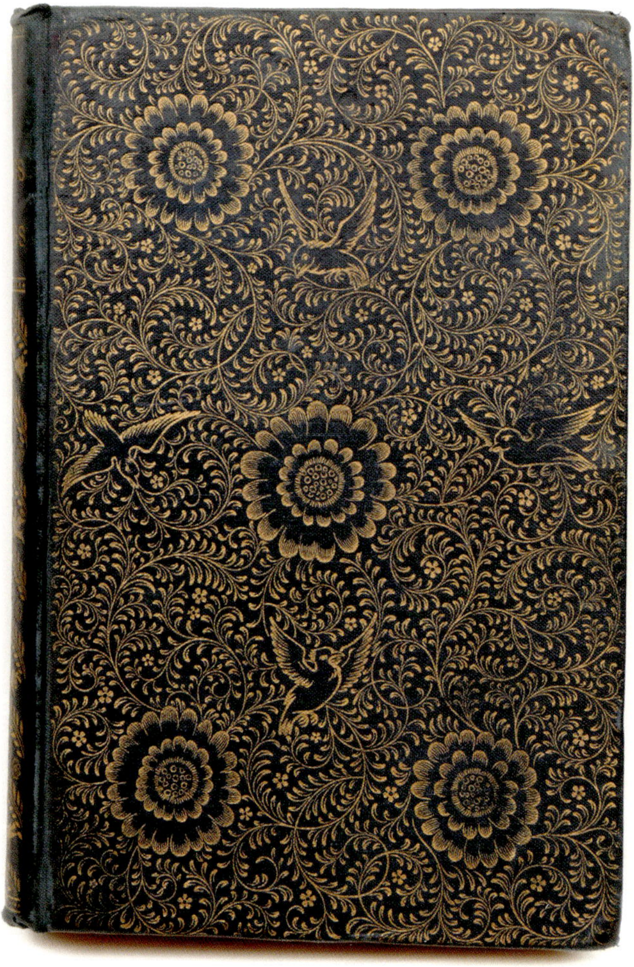

William Morris and Eiríkr Magnússon (trans.), *The Story of the Volsungs and Niblungs.* Cloth binding with stamped gold pattern designed by Philip Webb. First edition, 1870. Published by F. S. Ellis. William Morris Gallery, London.

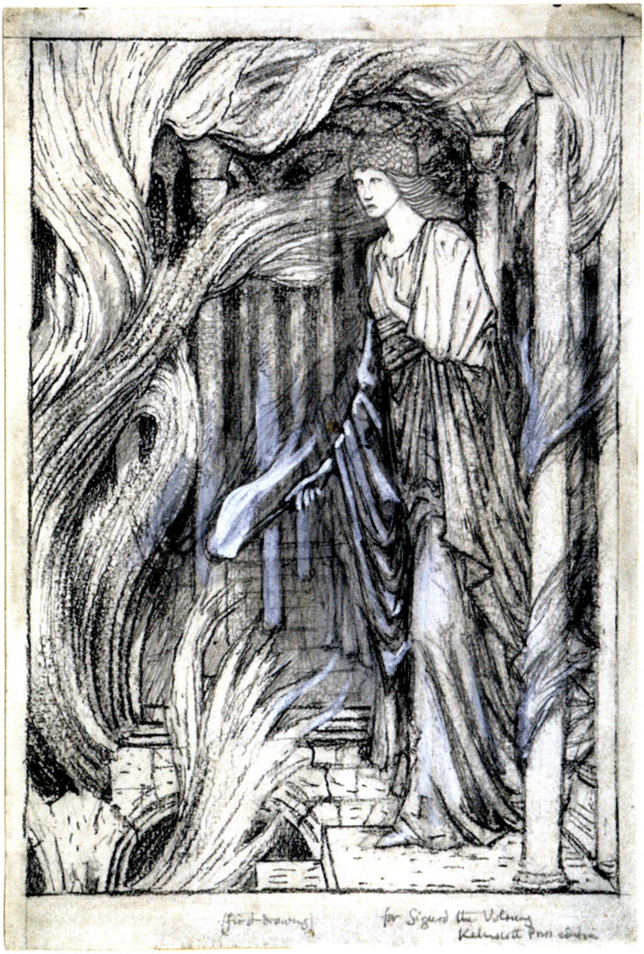

Edward Burne-Jones, *Gudrun Setting Fire to the House of King Atli*, sketch for illustration to *The Story of Sigurd the Volsung and the Fall of the Niblungs* by William Morris. Chalk and white on paper, 1898. William Morris Gallery, London.

William Morris, Ford Madox Brown, Edward Burne-Jones, Dante Gabriel Rossetti and Philip Webb, *The Labours of the Months* tiles.
Hand-painted on tin-glazed earthenware Dutch blanks. 31 x 83 cm each tile panel. 1863.
Painted by Lucy Faulkner for Morris, Marshall, Faulkner & Company.
William Morris Gallery, London.
Purchased with support from the MGC/V&A Purchase Grant Fund, the N.H.M.F, Friends of the William Morris Gallery and Walthamstow Historical Society.

Icelandic Sagas

William Morris and Eiríkr Magnússon (trans.), *The Story of the Volsungs and Niblungs.*
Cloth binding with stamped gold pattern designed by Philip Webb.
19.8 x 14 cm leaf. First edition, 1870.
Published by F. S. Ellis.
William Morris Gallery, London.

Edward Burne-Jones, *Gudrun Setting Fire to the House of King Atli,* sketch for illustration to *The Story of Sigurd the Volsung and the Fall of the Niblungs* by William Morris.
Chalk and white on paper. 51 x 37 cm. 1898.
William Morris Gallery, London.

William Morris, with illustrations by Edward Burne-Jones,
The Story of Sigurd the Volsung and the Fall of the Niblungs.
Paper with vellum binding. 32.2 x 23.5 cm leaf. 1898.
Kelmscott Press.
William Morris Gallery, London.

William Morris Gallery

"William Morris has taught me so much – about politics, about nature, about beauty, about poetry, about the role of art in the life of the people."

Clive Wilmer, poet, lecturer and Honorary Patron of the William Morris Gallery

The William Morris Gallery in Walthamstow, north-east London, is the only public gallery in the world devoted to the life, works and legacy of William Morris. The Gallery contains one of the most important collections of Morris's work, and is housed in a substantial Georgian dwelling that was the Morris's family home from 1848 to 1856. The house – known to Morris as Water House – was built in 1740; William Morris lived there from the age of fourteen to twenty-two with his widowed mother and eight brothers and sisters. The Morris children used the garden moat for boating and fishing in summer, and for ice-skating in winter. William Morris wrote some of his earliest poetry seated in the tall window on the main staircase, and his friend Edward Burne-Jones, on a visit to the Morris family in the 1850s, painted studies of the trees on the island.

When the Morris family left the house in 1856, its next occupant was the publisher Edward Lloyd (1815-1890), the proprietor of Lloyd's Weekly London Newspaper and of The Daily Chronicle. The Lloyd family donated the house and grounds to the people of Walthamstow and 'Lloyd Park' was opened in July 1900.

Plans to establish a Gallery dedicated to William Morris were formulated in 1935 but it was not until 1950 that the William Morris

Gallery was opened by the Prime Minister, Clement Attlee. One of the Gallery's first visitors was H.M. Queen Mary, whose husband George V had given Morris & Co. the Royal Warrant for its contributions to the 1911 Coronation.

The William Morris Gallery offers unparalleled resources for researching and telling the story of Morris's achievements and legacy. The collection represents William Morris, his family and close associates, including a wide range of Morris's detailed original designs and Morris & Co products, including wallpaper, woven and printed textiles, carpets, embroideries, tapestries, furniture and metalwork.

The Gallery also holds works by Sir Frank Brangwyn, RA, who served an apprenticeship with Morris, and material relating to The Century Guild and the wider Arts and Crafts Movement. Brangwyn and his fellow artist Arthur Mackmurdo were instrumental in setting up the gallery, and in turn presented a large part of their personal collections of 19th and early 20th century art to the Gallery, to serve as a memorial to the achievements of Morris and those who worked with him. In recognition of this, the full name of the gallery is 'The William Morris Gallery and Brangwyn Gift'.

The William Morris Gallery Development Project is the culmination of a longstanding ambition to remodel the Grade II* Listed building to enable it to fulfil its true potential. The £5m project will see the historic building refurbished and fully accessible with an extension on the site of the former east wing providing a new temporary exhibition space, conditioned object store and tearoom.

All permanent displays will be completely redesigned; visitors will explore Morris's story from his early years in Walthamstow, through to his achievements as a designer and the successes of Morris & Co. Hands-on, interactive exhibits will explore how products were designed, made and sold. New galleries will introduce the Kelmscott Press and Morris's radical campaigns for equality and the environment with items from the Brangwyn and Arts and Crafts collections highlighted in regularly changing displays.

Morris's legacy, in the widest sense, will be explored through an ambitious temporary exhibition programme encompassing historical displays and contemporary art, craft and design practice. Exciting activities, events and education programmes will also complement the new Gallery to attract more local people as well as those from elsewhere in the UK and abroad. The refurbished Gallery will reopen in July 2012.

The William Morris Gallery Development Project has been made possible through the generous support of the Heritage Lottery Fund and the London Borough of Waltham Forest. The William Morris Gallery is also extremely grateful for grants from numerous trusts, foundations and individuals, and The Friends of the William Morris Gallery.

William Morris Gallery

Waltham Forest

heritage lottery fund

Morris & Co. – A Revolution in Decoration
150 Years of Arts & Crafts design

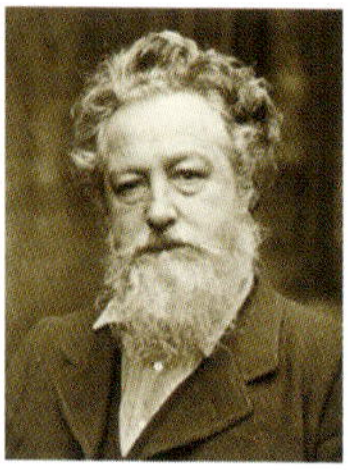

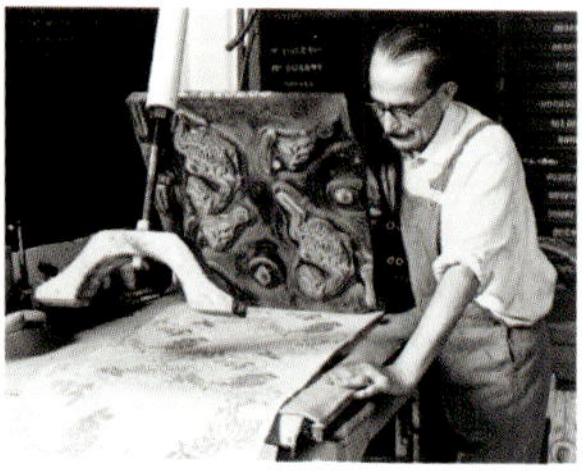

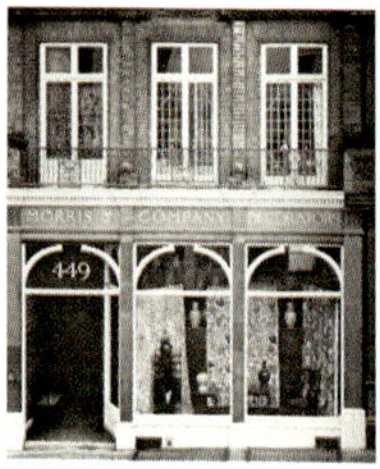

2011 sees the 150th anniversary of the founding of Morris, Marshall, Faulkner & Co. later to become Morris & Co., renowned globally for its distinctive style. 'The Firm' aimed to create the finest hand-made fabrics, wallpapers and furnishings at competitive prices - something that was considered controversial at the time. The founding of this company is an important landmark in British design history as the then vogue for opulent interiors had previously dominated Victorian style. Morris' hand-crafted design aesthetic was a revolution in decoration.

The stature of William Morris has grown throughout the 20th century. His work is synonymous with excellence of design and his legacy is reflected in the continuous demand for Arts & Crafts wallpapers and fabrics to this day.

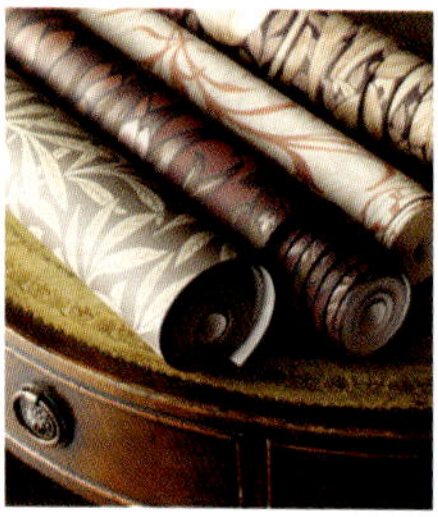

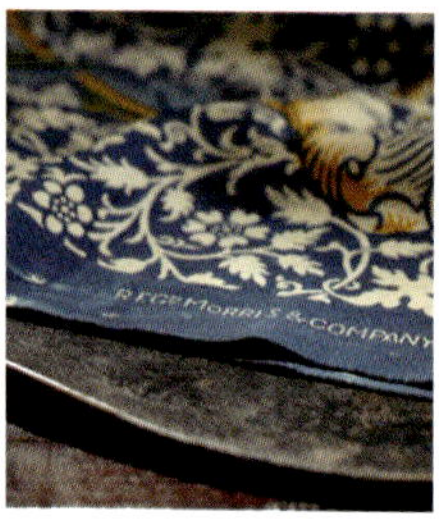

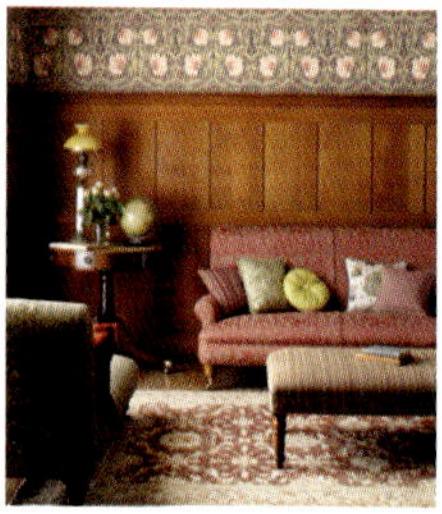

The Morris Years 1834-2011

1834	William Morris is born
1859	William Morris marries Jane Burden. Red House is designed and built for the Morris'
1861	Morris, Marshall, Faulkner & Co. is founded
1864	Morris designs his first 3 wallpaper patterns, 'Daisy', 'Trellis' & 'Fruit'
Late 1860s	Creates 'The Earthly Paradise'
1875	Relaunches the business as 'Morris & Co.'
1877	Opens shop and showroom at 449 Oxford Street
1881	Morris relocates his workshops to Merton Abbey
1880s	Morris joins the Socialist League
1890	J H Dearle takes over and runs Merton Abbey factory
1891	Kelmscott Press is founded
1896	William Morris dies
1905	Company renamed Morris & Co. Decorators Ltd
1920s	Most of Merton Abbey closes
1925	Company renamed Morris & Co. Art Workers Ltd
1926/1927	Sanderson takes over Jeffrey & Co manufacturing all the Morris & Co. block printed wallpapers
1940	Company goes into liquidation and is purchased by Arthur Sanderson & Sons Ltd
1950s	Sanderson relaunch Morris block printed wallpaper
1960	Sanderson launch "new" Morris fabrics
1965	Sanderson and Morris & Co. relaunched in Japan
1970s	Morris fabrics become popular again
1985	The first branded Morris & Co. collection is issued since Sanderson purchased the company 45 years earlier
1996	The Morris & Co. brand is re-established
2011	Morris & Co. celebrates its 150th Anniversary

Two Temple Place is wholly owned
by The Bulldog Trust

The Bulldog Trust

The Bulldog Trust Ltd
2 Temple Place
London
WC2R 3BD
www.bulldogtrust.org

Registered Charity Number 1123081
Registered Company Number 6510777